90 0807891 9

KW-467-147

This book is to be returned on
or before the date stamped below

22. FEB. 1993

15. DEC. 1993

26. APR. 1996 CANCELLED

1 6 APR 2004

POLYTECHNIC SOUTH WEST

ACADEMIC SERVICES
Plymouth Library
Tel: (0752) 232323
This book is subject to recall if required by another reader
Books may be renewed by phone
CHARGES WILL BE MADE FOR OVERDUE BOOKS

A book may be renewed by telephone or by personal visit
if it is not required by another reader.
CHARGES WILL BE MADE FOR OVERDUE BOOKS

WITHDRAWN
FROM
UNIVERSITY OF PLYMOUTH
LIBRARY SERVICES

PLYMOUTH
POLYTECHNIC
LIBRARY

PLYMOUTH POLYTECHNIC
LEARNING RESOURCES CENTRE

ACCN.

No.   22016

CLASS 335.50942 Soc
No.

-0. SEP. 1977

cover design and typography by Geoffrey Cannon. Printed by Civic Press Limited (TU), Civic Street, Glasgow, C4.

socialism and affluence

this book, like all publications of the Fabian Society, represents not the collective view of the Society but only the view of the individuals who prepared it. The responsibility of the Society is limited to approving the publications which it issues as worthy of consideration within the Labour movement.
Fabian Society, 11 Dartmouth Street, London SW1. May 1967
reprinted February 1970   SBN 7163 4002 X

the authors

William Rodgers

William Rodgers is Chairman of the Fabian Society and Parliamentary Under-Secretary for Foreign Affairs. He was General Secretary of the Fabian Society from 1953 to 1960 and wrote *What shall we do about the roads?* (Fabian research series 206).

Brian Abel-Smith

Brian Abel-Smith is Professor of Social Administration at the London School of Economics and Political Science and Honorary Treasurer and a former Chairman of the Fabian Society. He is author of *The Reform of Social Security* (Fabian research series 161), *Freedom in the Welfare State* (Fabian tract 352) and (jointly with Peter Townsend) *New Pensions for Old* (Fabian research series 171).

Richard M. Titmuss

Richard M. Titmuss, is Professor of Social Administration at the London School of Economics and Political Science. He is the author of *Essays on "the welfare state," Income distribution and social change, The irresponsible society* (Fabian tract 323) *Problems of social policy*, and other works. He would like to thank Michael Reddin, Brian Abel-Smith, Ann and Robin Oakley for comments on the draft of his essay.

Peter Townsend

Peter Townsend is Professor of Sociology at the University of Essex, and was Chairman of the Fabian Society in 1966. He is author of *The last refuge* (Routledge and Kegan Paul); *The family life of old people* (Routledge and Kegan Paul) and jointly with Brian Abel-Smith *New pensions for old* (Fabian research series 171). He would like to thank the following, for advice and help in the preparation of his essay: Brian Abel-Smith, Audrey Harvey, Hilary Land, Tony Lynes, Dennis Marsden, Adrian Sinfield, Richard Titmuss and John Veit Wilson.

R. H. S. Crossman

R. H. S. Crossman is Lord President of the Council and Leader of the House of Commons. He is author of *Socialism and the new despotism* (Fabian tract 298) and *Labour in the affluent society* (Fabian tract 325) and edited *New Fabian essays*.

introduction

William Rodgers

The Fabian Society, in the words of its constitution, "consists of socialists." This, perhaps, bold assumption is virtually the limit of its collective ideological commitment. There is no Fabian orthodoxy, no "line" which the Society is obliged to follow.

On the other hand, the Fabian Society is affiliated to the Labour Party, which it helped to create. Many of its members are active in the Labour movement. They helped the Labour Government to power in 1964 and again in 1966. They want to keep it there.

This dual loyalty to intellectual freedom and the Labour Party gives the Society a very special role. It must provide a forum for comment on Labour's record and intentions within a framework of sympathy and support. This involves the often uncomfortable obligations of the candid friend.

The following group of, four essays, originally given as lectures before a Fabian audience in the autumn of 1966, shows the Society performing this function at its best. These lectures, by Fabians of distinguished academic standing, are frankly critical of Labour's record and strategy in social policy. The fourth, by a Fabian member of the Cabinet, is a vigorous reply which also seeks to show the limitations of power.

This book is important not only as an example of the Fabian method and for the issues with which it deals. It shows how thoughtful socialists experiencing policy-making from different standpoints—from the outside in the Universities and the inside in government—can draw apart and misunderstand each other. This reason alone makes a continuing dialogue of this kind essential if harmony in creative achievement between politicians and academics is to be carried over from the barren years of opposition into the fruitful period ahead.

Labour's social plans

Brian Abel-Smith

What is Socialism about in the nineteen-sixties ? An answer can be found from the works of two leading members of the Labour cabinet. In the opening words of *The Conservative Enemy*, Tony Crosland gives us his unambiguous answer.

" Today we all accept some communal responsibility for overcoming poverty, distress and social squalor. The question is whether we do so gladly or grudgingly, and what priority we give it. A Socialist is identified as one who wishes to give this an exceptional priority over other claims on resources. . . . This represents the first major difference between a socialist and a conservative." (C. A. R. Crosland, *The Conservative Enemy*, p11, Jonathan Cape, 1962) In his book, Crosland condemned the widespread poverty and distress " amongst non-producing dependents and those with exceptionally heavy responsibilities—the sick, the widowed, those with large families and above all the two and a half million old people living below or near the poverty line." He particularly stressed the plight of " certain small groups with no electoral bargaining power "—the homeless, the chronic sick, problem families and most of all " those afflicted by several disabilities at once, such as solitary old people, disabled by physical or mental illness, yet still imprisoned in slum houses." He drew attention to the deficiences in our social capital : " the old age and dispiriting bleakness of most of our hospitals, the hopelessly overcrowded classes in many state schools, the shortage of university places, the uncivilised conditions in mental hospitals."

" These deficiences have come to seem the more vulgar as the general level of prosperity has risen. The large increase in conspicuous private goods such as cars and household durables : the growth of ostentatious private office-building; the growth of the teenage market. . . . We are now rich enough for the uncivilised state of the social sector, so deadening to happiness and vitality to stand out as unendurable." (*ibid*, p2) " The balance between public and private spending is wrong," Crosland told us. " We shall not put matters right unless we increase the proportion of the national income devoted to social purposes."

Douglas Jay in his *Socialism in the New Society*, published in the same year developed the same theme. " We are asked to believe by the extremer forms of propaganda that additional supplies of goods which minister to private spending are an access to national wealth and prosperity while almost any improvement of public services is a national extravagance." (Douglas Jay, *Socialism in the New Society*, p217, Longmans, 1962) Under this " crazy doctrine, the building of houses for those who need them but cannot pay for them is extravagant, but the building of houses for those who can pay for them, but may not need them is a growth of national wealth." He concluded that " the supply of any service is an addition to the national wealth if it meets a need, and is efficiently organised, entirely regardless of whether a public or private agency is responsible."

8

Owing to the crazy doctrines which had governed policy in the past and for other reasons there was a "continuous starvation of the public services." (*ibid*, p221) Bluntly he told us "Government and local authority expenditure . . . has always been too low: is too low today and ought to be increased." (*ibid*, p222) He argued therefore that "the assault on poverty and inequality through redistribution must remain the prime purpose for a very long time ahead." (*ibid*, p224) And in this assault it was necessary to avoid social discrimination "as far as possible." (*ibid*, p226) Secondly there were too few houses at rents people could afford. (*ibid*, p230) Thirdly, "the prime need is for British governments to stop starving our State educational system of the finance it needs to develop properly." (*ibid*, p245) The share of national resources going to education had to be increased. Fourthly, health and medical care were also "grievously starved of resources." (*ibid*, p252) Fifthly, "family allowances needed developing." (*ibid*, p253)

The thinking of Crosland and Jay and of many others who did not express their views in book form was reflected in the Labour Party home policy statement of 1961—*Signposts for the Sixties*. The statement identified the causes of Britain's decline. One of them was "the contrast between starved community services and extravagant consumption summed up . . . in the phrase, "private affluence and public squalor." It stated unequivocally, "One of the characteristics of the ever more complex civilisation in which we live is the need it imposes on the modern state to allocate more and more of the national resources to community services—health, education, social security and transport." (p8) I repeat "more and more of the national resources"—a higher proportion.

Since the early nineteen sixties the shortcomings of what the 1961 policy statement called the "community services" have become increasingly apparent. More and more information has become available from both public and private sources indicating serious shortages of services in general, chronic maldistribution of such services as were provided between different areas, and the extent to which Britain's Social Services have fallen behind those of other advanced nations.

education

The Newsom Report indicated the serious inadequacies of two-fifths of the schools for the age group 13-16 which it studied. (*Half Our Future*, HMSO, 1963) It called for an accelerated building programme, the raising of the school leaving age to 16 and a variety of other improvements, many of which entailed increased expenditure.

In the field of higher education the Robbins Committee showed university expansion had not "even quite kept pace with the increase in the age group, let alone the increase in the number of those with the minimum qualifications for entrance. (*Higher Education*, p12, Cmnd 2154, HMSO, 1963) The report showed on various assumptions that the proportion of national resources devoted to higher education would need to double between 1962 and 1980. (*ibid*, p208) It is likely that the Plowden Committee which is about to report on primary education will also point out in clear statistical terms the need for higher expenditure in the last main sector of education to be given a systematic post-war investigation—the primary schools.

In the health service official acceptance of the problem of the emigration of doctors and study of the implications of population changes on medical manpower have shown the need for a massive increase in medical education. Meanwhile ways and means have been found to give financial assistance to family doctors to enable them to give a better service by improving their premises and employing secretaries. The first national plan for community care showed the incredibly wide variations in the extent to which home helps, district nurses and health visitors were available in different areas. (*Health and Welfare*, Cmnd 1973, HMSO, 1963) As regards the hospital service, there have been growing complaints in the *British Medical Journal* and elsewhere about cross infection in operating theatres, about shocking conditions in psychiatric hospitals and the continuous lack of money to provide patients with the standard of care they are entitled to expect.

social security

In the social security sector, the Ministry of Pensions and National Insurance finally confirmed from its own somewhat belated study of the aged (*Financial and other Circumstances of Retirement Pensioners*, HMSO, 1963) what Peter Townsend and Dorothy Wedderburn had shown from their own studies over a period of ten years that there is a massive problem of recipients of national insurance benefit failing to apply for supplementary national assistance. (Peter Townsend, *The Family Life of Old People*, Routledge, 1957; Dorothy Cole, *The Economic Circumstances of Old People*, Bell, 1962; Peter Townsend and Dorothy Wedderburn, *The Aged in the Welfare State*, Bell 1965) Allowing for all categories entitled to receive assistance there are roughly a million people below the basic national assistance level of living who are entitled to but do not apply for help.

Pressure from academics and Labour members has forced the department to look into the effects of the wage stop regulations and reveal the fact that a third of the unemployed with children who were receiving assistance were subject to this cruel regulation. The laws of the Welfare State still provide no means by which such families can obtain the basic minimum widely believed to be available to the whole population. In addition there is the vast problem of families where earnings from full-time work are not adequate to raise the family above assistance level. (Brian Abel-Smith and Peter Townsend, *The Poor and the Poorest,* Bell, 1965)

As a result of all this new research, the fact that poverty is widespread in Britain is now accepted as it has never been since pre-war days. The dailies and the weeklies, sound broadcasts and television shows periodically remind the public of the seven and a half million persons, two and a quarter million of them children, at or around the national assistance level of living of which two million persons, 700,000 of them children, below the crude national assistance scales in 1960. At the lower end of the income scale if not also at the higher end inequality appears to be increasing. The word poverty, applied to affluent Britain, is now rehabilitated to find a regular place in the leader-writer's copy.

SOCIAL POLICY AND THE NATIONAL PLAN

While Crosland and Jay and the authors of *Signposts for the Sixties* had good reason for demanding in the early sixties that more resources should be devoted to the social services, the accumulating evidence of the last four years has greatly strengthened their case. A socialist, as Crosland has told us, is a person who gives exceptional priority to overcoming poverty, distress and social squalor over other claims on resources. Taking this as our text, let us review the social planning of the Labour Government. Though the economic difficulties of the last year have made the National Plan sadly out of date, the original document published over a year ago provides the most detailed picture of the government's approach to long term planning. Taking the investment sector first, manufacturing and construction was to increase by $7\frac{1}{2}$ per cent per annum on average over the period of the plan. Public service investment (excluding roads and housing) was to increase by under 7 per cent per annum and housing by under 5 per cent per annum. On the consumption side social and other public services were to increase by 4 per cent per annum and personal private consumption by 3.2 per cent per annum. Public services were to grow at a slightly faster rate than private consumption. However the latter was in 1964 the largest single user of national resources. Thus out of a planned increase of £8,200 million in the gross national product, £4,400 million (over half) was to go in personal consumption. (*The National Plan,* p161, Cmnd 2764, HMSO, 1965)

It seems important however to see how the rate of increase in the public services projected in the plan compares with earlier trends. Moreover as the plan involves giving a greater weight for public housing as opposed to private housing it seems also relevant, when making any comparisons with the past, to consider housing investment as a whole. The blue book, *National Income and Expenditure,* 1965, does show estimates for public expenditure in constant prices for past years. How does the distribution of resources for the six years 1958 to 1964 compare with that planned for the six years 1964 to 1970? The two tables below cover public current expenditure on goods and services excluding defence and total investment (public and private) on housing.

EXPENDITURE AT 1958 PRICES (£ million)

	1958	1964
private investment in housing	322	625
public investment in housing	269	463
national health service	694	813
education	553	697
other	960	1,165
total	2,798	3,763

source : *National Income and Expenditure*, 1965, pp 19, 63.

EXPENDITURE AT 1964 PRICES (£ million)

	1964	1970
housing	1,209	1,595
social and other public services	3,481	4,405
total	4,690	6,000

source : *The National Plan*, p161.

The calculation shows that the public services (current) and housing increased by 34.5 per cent in constant prices between 1958 and 1964 and are planned to increase by only 28 per cent between 1964 and 1970. Thus the absolute rate of growth was greater in the six years preceding 1964 than in the six years planned from 1964 onwards.

The plan provides for about the same overall rate of growth of the economy between 1964 and 1970—of 25 per cent compared with an achieved growth of 25.4 per cent between 1959 and 1964. Whereas the plan provides for an increase of personal consumption of 21 per cent between 1964 and 1970 personal consumption actually rose in real terms by 23 per cent between 1958 and 1964. Thus Labour's plan gives more relative weight to personal consumption compared with public services and housing than the Tories during the last six years of their administration. Or to put it another way, the gap between private spending and " social " spending narrowed faster under the Tories than under Labour's plan for the future.

This comparison is subject to two qualifications. First, much depends on the years of Tory rule brought into the comparison. There was a sharp increase in expenditure between 1963 and the " boom " year 1964. Secondly, the table does not include all the " social services," as comparable figures for the whole public social services are not available. It would be helpful if the full set of figures in the plan could be compared with the pre-plan experience. But nevertheless I would conclude that a man from Mars given Crosland's definition of socialism and the official statistics might easily make a mistake in an attempt to identify the socialist party. The general point which needs to be made is not just a statistical quibble. It is this : *The National Plan* makes extraordinarily little provision for narrowing the gap between private affluence and public squalor.

housing

Let us consider the implications of the plan in the various parts of the social programme. First, let us consider housing. The plan provided for an increase in the annual rate of investment in housing (public and private) of 32 per cent between 1964 and 1970. This compares with an achieved increase of 84 per cent in the period 1958 to 1964. At first sight a target of 500,000 houses built by 1970 sounds impressive. But after allowing for losses of houses to make way for other developments and provision for new household formation, the remaining part of the five year plan allows us to replace existing houses at the rate of about $1\frac{1}{2}$ per cent per annum. The fact that 17 per cent of our existing houses are believed to need replacement, including over 5 per cent of houses officially designated as slums, brings the plan into perspective. (*The National Plan*, p172) Nor is the strain which Britain's planned housing programme will make upon our national resources a world record. In 1970, 3.9 per cent of gross national product is planned to be spent on housing construction. As an average, for the years 1954 to 1958 New Zealand, Greece, and Switzerland were spending nearly 5 per cent of gross domestic product on housing : Sweden and Italy were spending around $5\frac{1}{2}$ per cent; a three year average for Israel was as high as $7\frac{1}{2}$ per cent. (*Report on the World Social Situation*, p67, United Nations, New York, 1961) Few would lay bets that 500,000 houses will actually be built in 1970 : but a long term target of 750,000 houses is not impossible in view of what other countries have achieved.

health and education

Current expenditure on the health service is planned to increase by 18 per cent between 1964/65 and 1969/70. (*The National Plan*, p185) This compares favourably with an increase of 13 per cent between 1959 and 1964. The abolition of the prescription charge has however absorbed roughly a quarter of the increased expenditure, making the planned growth in total expenditure on health much the same as under the Tories. As the proportion of the national product devoted to health services was about the same when the Labour government returned to office as in the first full year of the health service, this means that it is planned that about the same proportion of gross national product will be spent on health services over a full twenty year period. This completely contradicts international experience.

In every other high income country for which data is available, an extra one to two per cent of gross national product is devoted to health services every ten years. (*Royal Commission on Health Services*, p482, Queen's Printer, Ottawa, 1964) Public and private expenditure on health services was a little over 4 per cent of gross national product in 1949. If expansion had been at the same rate as in other countries we would be planning to spend at least 6½ per cent of gross national product by 1970, the figure achieved by Canada in 1961, and likely to be achieved by the United States this year. (*ibid*, p425)

In criticism of this, it may be said that comparisons with the United States and Canada are unfair as both these countries have large private sectors. But they are the only countries for which published information on total expenditure (public and private) on health services are available. If, however, we confine comparisons to public expenditure on health, it is of interest to note that the percentage of national income spent on current public health services in 1962 was 4.0 per cent in the United Kingdom, 4.1 per cent in Norway, 4.6 per cent in Denmark and 4.8 per cent in Sweden. (*Social Security in Nordic Countries*, Oslo, 1965) If we were in line with Sweden, Britain would be spending over £200 million more on its health service. I do not want to spell out what this really means in terms of poor amenities and less than the best medical care for patients. But it should be appreciated that the general standard of our health service is rapidly falling behind that of other advanced nations.

The bulk of capital in the health service inevitably goes on hospitals. The plan points out the, by now familiar, fact that half the hospitals inherited by the national health service were built in the last century and many are over 100 years old. (*The National Plan*, p186) Little building has taken place in the last eighteen years. The vast majority of our hospitals are ill designed and wrongly sited. Moreover in no social field does plant become obsolete so quickly. Changes in medical practice have totally transformed the type of building needed for a hospital over the past 40 years. After allowing for the increase in hospital facilities needed to meet the needs of the growing population, the existing rate of hospital construction as described in *The Hospital Building Programme* (Cmnd 3000, HMSO, 1966) would succeed in replacing our hospitals in 100 years. The plan provides for this period to be reduced to 60 years by 1970. But in practice a considerable part of the allotted capital funds will have to be used to patch up the old buildings to keep them in use until their turn comes for replacement.

In the case of education the possibilities are to a certain extent limited by the rate

14

at which the teaching profession can be expanded. It is not possible from the information available to compare the rate of growth with that experienced in the past, but it is probably greater. The plan provides for teachers to increase faster than pupils so that the pupil teacher ratio will improve by around 5 per cent before the strain on resources of raising the school leaving age has been taken up soon after 1970. Little surplus for upgrading and replacement of unsatisfactory schools is left after provision has been made for the increase in the number of school children. The plan leaves little scope for facilitating the growth of comprehensive schools by new construction.

The extent of planned progress in the health and education sectors of the plan can be seen from the bald statement about the allocation of manpower to these sectors. " In the case of health and education the forecast rate (of growth of manpower) is approximately 1 per cent a year slower than in recent years, even though increasing demands on these services will have to be met." In other words health and education manpower will expand at a slower rate under Labour than under the Tories.

social security

The allocation for higher social security benefits is an increase of 15 per cent after allowance has been made for the natural increase in persons entitled to benefits—more aged persons entitled to pensions, more children entitled to family allowances, etc. As the plan (p66) provides for wages to increase by 21 per cent (taking the mid point between 3 per cent and $3\frac{1}{2}$ per cent per annum) it is apparently intended, even without any extension in the scope of social security, that the level of living of social security beneficiaries will fall behind that of wage earners. Social dependents are not to receive their share of national prosperity, as £68 million is allotted to wage related sickness and unemployment benefits and a further sum to expenditure arising out of the reform of National Assistance, these developments must be achieved at the cost of widening the gap between benefit and wages for those not benefiting from these particular programmes.

The allocation to social security has been kept extraordinarily low although a recent study has pointed out that " the proportion of national resources devoted to social security (in Britain) is very much lower than in any of the Common Market countries." It is worth reciting the figures on the basis of which this statement was made. In 1960, the proportion of gross national product going to social cash benefits in the United Kingdom was 6.4 per cent. The corresponding figures for other countries were Denmark 6.8 per cent, New Zealand 7.2 per cent, Netherlands 7.7 per cent, Italy 7.9 per cent, France 8.3 per cent, Belgium 8.8 per cent, Sweden 9.1 per cent, Austria 9.2 per cent, West Germany 10.4 per cent. The report added that " one of the weakest elements in the social security system of this country is the provision for family allowances. They are much lower than in other countries which provide them." Again it is worth quoting the statistics. A four child family in Britain received family allowances worth 13 per cent of national income per head of working population. In the Netherlands and Western Germany this proportion was 25 per cent, in Belgium 45 per cent, in Italy 54 per cent, in France 63 per cent. (" Social Security in Britain and certain other countries," *National Institute Economic Review*, no. 33, August 1965)

If it were decided to raise family allowances to the level of living recommended in the Beveridge Report (in other words correcting for price changes since the report was written) this would absorb virtually the whole of the social security allocation. It is tempting to drive the point home by repeating the categories for which Crosland showed particular sympathy. The mean allocation for social security, the persistence of the wage stop, of unreasonable rent cases and most important of all the persistence of inadequate family allowances which in itself ensures that over half a million persons (most of them children) are below crude assistance level squares unhappily with one of Mr. Wilson's TV election broadcasts. On 23 September 1964, he told the nation : " What we are going to do now—we are going to do it early because it is urgent in the first few weeks of a Labour Government—is to provide a guaranteed income below which no one will be allowed to fall." (quoted in James and Audrey Kincaid, " The Glossy Soup Kitchen," *International Socialism,* Summer 1966, p10)

is this socialism ?

Thus in general *The National Plan* makes extraordinarily low provision for improvements in the social services. In reply to this criticism of the low priority accorded to what it is now fashionable to call social development as against economic development, it can fairly be said that the main purpose of the plan was to straighten out our economic difficulties. The plan states this very clearly. " The task of correcting the balance of payments and achieving the surplus necessary to repay our debts, while at the same time fostering the rapid growth of the economy, is the central challenge. We must succeed if we are to achieve all our objectives of social justice and welfare, of rising standards of living, of better social capital, and of a full life for all in a pleasant environment." (p1)

While it is undoubtedly true that correcting the balance of payments is an essential aim and that failing to do so could lead to mass unemployment, it is by no means certain that social justice, welfare and better social capital depend upon rapid growth of the economy. The ugly gap between private affluence and public squalor could be corrected without rapid economic growth—indeed considerable progress could be made without any economic growth at all. Are we really so selfish as a Society that we are saying to all the people in need whom Tony Crosland has named, " We won't sacrifice any of our existing private affluence to help you. All we can do is to promise you a share—indeed, a pathetically small share of any new affluence "—if it comes.

It is a terrifying fallacy to pretend that economic and social aims are wholly competitive. Why do we want economic growth if it is not to promote social and not economic ends—higher levels of living whether they are gained through collective provision or private provision. In planning for developing countries it is at last recognised that economic and social objectives are not competing ends but that all ends are social and that economic development is only one of the means. (*Social and Economic Factors in Development,* pp 12-13, UNRISD, Geneva, 1966)

The national plan aimed to increase output by £8,000 million over six years. The plan stated that out of this, £2,000 million was needed to correct the balance of payments and to increase investment in private and nationalised industry. Out of the remaining £6,000 million over £500 million was set aside for housing and roads. This left less than £5,500 million to be divided between private affluence and public squalor on current account. The plan gave less than £1,000 million to public squalor and nearly £4,500 million to private affluence. Is this Socialism? It is time that now that growth is now sadly off target, social expenditure has on the whole been kept as planned with the result that the cut is falling on private investment and private consumption. But it is hardly satisfactory to define a socialist as someone who preserves the social services when times are hard.

WHY LIMIT SOCIAL SPENDING ?

In certain narrow fields there certainly can be competition between what is required to balance our payments and what is needed for the expansion of our social services. It may be that the capacity of the building industry will be stretched to the maximum by the combination of the 1970 planned construction of factories to expand exports, and the planned housing, school, university and hospital building programmes. But we want to be told categorically that the whole of the potential output of the building industry including the resources released by the check on office building will be taken up in these fields.

It may be true also that the rate of social development is held back by shortages of skilled personnel. This is certainly a major limiting factor in education. There is also a shortage of doctors. But much could be done by using lower grades of personnel under the supervision of professionals. Over the years doctors in hospitals have been only too glad to shed some of the jobs which do not need their scarce skills to trained auxiliaries and have gained enhanced status by leading teams of professional personnel instead of working in isolation. Dentists and teachers have been less cooperative in this respect. How long is society going to be held to ransom by the monopolistic restrictive practices of professional groups ? The restrictive practices of trade unions are chicken feed when compared to those of certain professional associations.

In many fields the social services are not held back by trained manpower shortages and in others, where they are, the cause can often be found in the shortage of training facilities—in the rate of expansion of higher education which is pathetically below the requirements of the nineteen-seventies and eighties. Staff could be found for the education, health and welfare services if less was used in advertising and in making luxury goods.

The point is clearest when one looks at the social security sector. Here it is not so much a question of public spending versus private spending but of whose private spending. Is the money better used enabling a mother of a large family to give her children a standard of living above subsistence level or enabling people to attend bunny clubs and gambling saloons ? This is the moral choice which any government has to make.

Why have we allowed ourselves to become enslaved to the cause of restraining public expenditure as if every extra penny handled by the government was a drain on our economic growth and a diversion from the export drive ? The absurdities of this thinking have been so clearly exposed by Douglas Jay that it is worth quoting some further sentences from the same source.

" The doctrine runs like this," he went on to declare, " ' Expenditure on cars is good and adds to the national wealth, because it is private. Expenditure on roads is national extravagance, beckoning us towards financial ruin, because it is public.' So we observe every fine week-end huge stationary jams of expensive private cars held up by road bottlenecks, which only public spending can cure. Or ' the building of private schools is a meritorious enterprise : the building of State schools is a waste of money.' So we find great private firms, with the help of tax rebates, constructing private schools, splendid science laboratories which the Government often declares to be too costly for State schools. . . . Or expenditure on medical care and equipment is scientific progress if privately financed : but is wicked Socialism if the same care and equipment is provided by a public authority for those most in need. The payment of pensions (so we are asked to believe) ' through private superannuation schemes, heavily subsidised by the State, is the height of prudence and sound finance. But the payment of pensions to those probably even more in need through a State scheme is extravagance likely to unbalance the national finances.' To such absurdities do the arguments in the end lead by which reactionaries today in every country try to resist the growth of the public services." (*Socialism in the New Society*, p217)

All splendid stuff. Yet *The National Plan* reads "The Government have been engaged in a thoroughgoing review of the whole field of public expenditure. Changes have been made to ensure that total planned expenditure is within our means." What does this mean—" within our means "? What determines the level of social spending ? This is one of the questions that Crosland asked and answered in *The Conservative Enemy*. " In a free society, the real limit is set by the proportion of income which the electors are willing to forego from individual spending." (p22) In other words it is a political limit. " Within our means " is a naughtily misleading way of saying that the Government has decided to allocate £1,000 million of new money to public consumption and £4,500 million to private consumption.

absurdities

The limit on public expenditure was fixed early in the Government's history. The figure of 4¼ per cent per year at constant prices was decided on in February 1965—long before the rest of the plan was put together. (*The National Plan*, p176) These are times when one has been tempted to believe that the foreign bankers who may well subscribe to what Douglas Jay called the " crazy doctrines " have imposed the tough public expenditure limit as the price for their support. But officially we are told that this is not so. It is also important to observe that the limit of 4¼ per cent was fixed before departmental Ministers had really had the time to take stock of the services they were controlling. Rightly, a battery of new enquiries were launched to ascertain need in a variety of forms and to study the effectiveness of particular services. There appears to be little flexibility within the system of public expenditure control by which the recognition of new needs can result in a reallocation not just of departmental resources but of national resources.

Thus we have excellent Ministers in charge of spending departments bound hand and foot by the confines of public expenditure and even defending the shabby features of our welfare state which they have long been attacking. Meanwhile the sectors of the Welfare State which lie outside the boundaries of public expenditure continue to progress from strength to strength. Occupational benefits—pensions, sick pay and the rest are subject to no restraint under the plan. With an increase in direct taxation the value of tax allowances is correspondingly increased. Among the higher income groups where income tax really matters, the fiscal advantages of being aged, having children, dependents and nannies are made greater. There are higher tax subsidies to private pensions schemes and members of BUPA. It becomes more advantageous to finance public school education through endowment policies and covenants.

But the greatest absurdities of controlling public expenditure, while turning a blind eye to tax allowances and private occupational social security, health and welfare benefits can be shown by a number of examples. If a law were passed which compelled employers as a condition of service to pay the existing state sickness and unemployment benefits to their emloyees, public expenditure would be reduced and new money released—presumably to the Minister of Social Security to spend on other benefits within the designated limits of public expenditure. If the existing inequitable tax allowances for children were paid out as cash benefits, two heinous sins would have been committed—higher taxation and higher public expenditure— indeed considerably more than the Minister of Social Security's quota for the full five years. If existing income tax payers were given their present cash family allowances in the form of higher income tax relief for children, the economic miracle would have been achieved of lower public expenditure and lowering taxation without making anyone worse off. It may well be said that those who control public expenditure would not tolerate such ways of wriggling round the system. But the important point is this. Public expenditure control limits intelligent discussion of related issues of social policy. Sickness benefit, pensions, etc., imposed by the Government are heavily restricted, pensions and sick pay imposed by employers are entirely free of any control. The Inland Revenue refuses to see itself as what it is—one of the principal agents for social security—and thus fails to coordinate its activities with the Ministry of Social Security. If people want some of their pay to be transferred to the sick and aged in return for a guarantee that they in turn will receive more when they are sick and aged, why should two mechanisms be approved (employers' schemes and tax concessions) and a third disapproved (transfer through the Ministry of Social Security)?

CHARGES AND MEANS TESTS

Corsetted within their financial quotas, it is not surprising that departmental Ministers should be tempted to try and find means of improving the standard of their services without exceeding their quotas. There are, as indeed there have always been, three possibilities. The first is to cut back some services to enable others to expand. The second is to introduce charges or increase existing charges. The third is to introduce some form of means test for particular services. In this last connection it should be pointed out that it is to some extent an historical accident that that the principle of universality has been applied to the main social security benefits and to health and education services but not to housing, welfare services, school meals, uniform grants, educational maintenance allowances, or maintenance allowances for higher education. The rationale of this deserves discussion, but this would take us far afield.

scope for further changes

It is often assumed that there is no scope for further charges in the social services which would be acceptable. But is this true ? In the health field there are a number of possibilities. First, under a law dating back to the early nineteen thirties hospitals can and do make charges for treatment arising as a result of road accidents. The scale of charges has not been revised since they were laid down in the original Act and are hopelessly below costs. It would be quite possible to charge the full cost of treating motor accidents. Most of cost would be absorbed in motor insurance policies and it seems just for motorists to be made to pay for the repair of the damage they have done to others. The principle might be extended to industrial accidents. Why should not the National Health Service bill employers for accidents " arising out of and in the course of employment." Of course the billing would involve administrative costs but the revenue would surely be sufficient to justify these costs. Secondly, if a time came when a modest inflationary pressure could be absorbed, employers might be required to pay the same contribution towards the National Health Service as their employees. This is the practice in much of Europe. The revenue from this would make it possible to more than double the hospital building programme—to name only one possible use of the money. Thirdly, why do private patients who use national health service hospitals pay less than the full cost. They are usually given more expensive food than other patients, more trained nurses are needed to service single rooms, and most important of all no element of depreciation or rent enters into the charges which they pay. In a new teaching hospital the latter would justify an extra charge of at least £10 a week—such is the cost of new hospital construction.

In the educational field there seems less scope for charges. One obvious step is to remove all the complicated hidden subsidies to the public schools. There is also a strong case for more realistic charges for university courses and a system of loans for university students should not be ruled out—though it would be many years before this brought any relief to the public purse.

ensuring services are available

This is not the place for a full discussion of the use of the means test in what are now universal services. But more and more conservative voices are echoing the thinking of the Institute of Economic Affairs and demanding a return to the market and the means test. This trend of thinking has occurred despite the fact that during the past five years evidence has been accumulating which shows that the means tests we have already do not work. For years it has been assumed that making a service available on a means test basis is sufficient for it to be used by those who need it. In almost no field is this true.

The failure of the National Assistance Board to reach all entitled to help has been mentioned above. The new Ministry of Social Security will undoubtedly improve this tragic situation but it will not solve it. For the assistance system to work people have to know their rights and be prepared to apply for them. There will remain many who do not know they can be helped and many who would rather go without than apply.

Miss Hilary Land has produced new data showing that many eligible large families do not get free school meals, uniform grants, holidays and educational maintenance allowances. Most local authorities take virtually no step to see that the terms upon which these services can be received are known to parents. Here is an extremely serious problem of children not receiving what they are entitled to. The value of these supplements to the living standards of a child can be as much as four times the value of family allowances. As yet, no way has been found of ensuring that services available on a test of means are received by those entitled to them. It is theoretically possible to solve this problem with cooperation from the Inland Revenue. But even this solution bristles with administrative difficulties. The assumption that problems of need can be solved immediately by a greater resort to the means test is naive, uniformed and at worst hypocritical.

vouchers for school meals

Instead of planning an extension of means tests, much more thought is needed to see that, where existing means tests operate, those who are entitled receive the services. Alternatively, the whole process of having a means test might be circumvented. This can be illustrated from one area of need—school meals. Some families prefer to pay for school meals rather than have their children branded as free meals children at school. In most schools free school meals children are known by their class-mates. At the worst schools there are two queues—one of children who pay and one of children who do not. The latter queue in some areas consists primarily of immigrant children. Surely the answer is to run the school meals service on a voucher basis with the vouchers being on sale at the Post Office.

They might be given free to all large families and included in the family allowance books issued to the mothers of these families. Other families in need could be given identical vouchers by the local authority. There seems no objection to the vouchers being exchanged for cash by families which did not wish to use the school meals service. This would by no means solve all the problems, but it would solve some.

WHY NOT RAISE TAXATION ?

There is, therefore, no case for trying to raise additional revenue for the social services by a greater use of means tests but there is some scope for further charges. But such charges could not bring in anything like enough revenue to plug the gap between private affluence and public squalor or to give a minimum of affluence to the millions of Britain's poor. We are back at the central dilemma. Are we prepared to reallocate not only new resources but also old resources on a sufficient scale to meet the need ? If a Labour Government won't, who will ? Socialists are often accused of wanting to level down instead of levelling up. Socialists are not afraid or should not be afraid of advocating redistributive policies. But it is irritating to hear conservatives using the " levelling up not down argument " to oppose change. In many respects socialism is about levelling up. This is precisely what our aim should be in health, education and social security.

We want to give everyone the costly education the wealthy enjoy, to give everyone the amenities that go with BUPA medical care, to give everyone the standard of social security provided under the best occupational schemes at the present time.

Where the transfer of resources to the social services takes place through government this inevitably involves higher taxation. What is wrong with that, providing the taxation is fair ? Yet we find the Governor of the Bank of England reported as saying that taxation is " already dangerously high." One wonders what Douglas Jay thought about that statement. Was this part of the " crazy doctrines " ? The Governor also told us that " now ' fiscal policy ' must mean further reduction in the growth of governmental spending, including with special emphasis that of the local authorities." As the *Economist* asked, " what precisely do Governor O'Brien and his likeminded friends have in mind " (29 October 1966.) He should not make such a statement unless he is prepared to come clean and make specific proposals. Does he want to cut expenditure on the police, on housing, on education, on sewerage, on refuse disposal or on the community care services so essential to the sick and frail ? Last year spending on educational building was actually down £5 million on the previous year.

Why should expenditure be cut ? Is this the old text book argument about incentives ? Whatever the conventional wisdom may say, such empirical research studies as there are give little support to the supposed general relation between taxation and incentives. In a scientific age we can no longer rely on general statements based on traditional theories. We want to know which taxpayers are proved to be affected by which taxes.

Britain lightly taxed

As a whole the most recent figures show Britain much more lightly taxed than our continental neighbours who, as a whole, have experienced much more favourable rates of economic growth than we have. In the United Kingdom taxes took 32.5 per cent of gross national product. The corresponding figures for Belgium were 32.9 per cent, for Italy 35.8 per cent, for the Netherlands 36.4 per cent, for West Germany 40.3 per cent, and for France 44.6 per cent. The main difference between us and our continental neighbours is in the role of social security contributions. We still have mainly a flat rate contribution system—a heavy weight of regressive taxation at the bottom of the tax structure and an inelastic source of revenue for social benefits. Such wage-related contributions as there are stop at a low income ceiling. The long awaited review of the whole social security system could be one of the keys to future progress in the Welfare State. But such a review is useless unless it is allowed to break through the whole of the public expenditure control system—to lay the Gladstonian ghost which still haunts the Treasury and the Bank of England.

tax changes

A second key to progress in the welfare state would be the abolition of tax allowances to all social dependents. This should form part of the social security review. Cash allowances must be substituted for allowances against income tax and the two existing social security systems—the Inland Revenue and the Ministry of Social Security—must be rationalised. At last, the quality press has taken up this cause : both *The Observer* leader writer and *The Times* Labour Correspondent have recently come out in favour of rationalising child allowances in the income tax with family allowances.

Any changes in taxes and social security contributions must of course take account of the tax system as a whole. In the same way as most people in Britain appear to believe that we have the highest taxation and the most generous social services in the world, so do most people appear to believe that the British tax system as a whole is progressive throughout its whole range—that the richer you are, the higher proportion of your income you pay in taxes of all kinds. This, however, is simply not true. Let us take as an example a family of two adults plus one child in 1962. The average taxes paid by households with an income of £500 per year was 37 per cent; where the household income was £1,100 per year, the proportion paid in taxes had dropped on average to under 28 per cent; even at £1,300 per year the burden of taxation was less than 30 per cent (calculated from Central Statistical Office, *New Contributions to Economic Statistics*, pp 104-22, Third Series, 1964) Because of the heavy burdens of national insurance contributions, rates and indirect taxes, low incomes in Britain are substantially more heavily taxed than average incomes. Only those with relatively high incomes pay as heavy taxes as those with low incomes. The middle income groups have long been the great mass of undertaxed in Britain.

It is too early yet to know the impact on the tax system of a Labour Government. The statistics are not yet available. National Insurance contributions have been increased, a massive extra weight has been thrown on the tax on cigarettes : the incidence of both these is heavily regressive. On the other hand, petrol has also been heavily hit, income tax has been increased and a capital gains tax has been introduced—though the effect of the latter in this present year is likely to help rather than harm the wealthy. In addition rate relief has been introduced though probably about half a million entitled persons have failed to claim. It will be interesting to see the total effect of all this. What has the government done to turn into legislation its statement in the 1964 election manifesto. " Taxation must be fair and must be seen to be fair." (*The New Britain*, pp 12-13)

conclusion

Much of this has been critical of Labour's social planning, but the criticism is intended to be constructive. It is true that the present economic crisis has been ignored in this discussion. But with luck, the crisis should be over in a few months and the government will be in a position to prepare a new national plan. And when it does so, let us hope that it will bear in mind that a Socialist is one who wishes to give the relief of poverty, distress and social squalor an exceptional priority over other claims on resources.

choice and "the welfare state"

Richard M. Titmuss

For those of us who are still socialists the development of socialist social policies in the next few years will represent one of the cardinal tests on which the Labour Government will be judged—and sternly judged—in the early 1970's. Economic growth, productivity and change are essential; about this there can be no dispute. But as we—as a society—become richer shall we become more equal in social, educational and material terms ? What does the rise of " affluence " spell to the values embodied in the notion of social welfare ?

For the purposes of this pamphlet I have, in asking these questions, to take a long view and disregard our immediate economic and social problems. One assumption I have to make is that over the next ten years (and thereafter) British society will be substantially richer; that, on average, the population of Britain will be living at a higher standard than today. In his pamphlet *Labour's social plans* (Fabian tract 369) Professor Abel-Smith dealt with what he called the " ugly imbalance between private affluence and public squalor," and went on to direct a searching attack on the social policy content of the Government's *National plan* (Cmnd 2764, HMSO, September 1965)

He assumed (as I do) that over the period of the *National plan* we may expect to be (in company with other highly industrialised countries of the West) a richer society in the 1970's. Now that the Government has begun to lay a sounder basis for a higher rate of growth in the future after inheriting a decade or more of incompetence and dereliction it is, I think, more rather than less likely that our economic targets will be broadly attained.

But, at the present time, economic and industrial policies are involving much hardship for a minority of workers; whether this was or was not inevitable is a matter on which a great deal more could be said, and no doubt will be said. The acid test will come, however, in the next few years; there will be many who will want to know by the time the life of this Government comes to its natural end whether those who are making sacrifices now in the general interest will be more than justly compensated.

This question of who should bear the social and economic costs of change is relevant to the larger issue of the future role of the social services in a more affluent society. First, however, let us remember the general thesis about " freedom of choice " now being forcefully presented by various schools of " liberal " economists in Britain, Western Germany and the United States—notably in the writings of Professor Friedman of Chicago and his friends and followers in London and elsewhere (M. Friedman, *Capitalism and Freedom*, University of Chicago Press, 1962) Broadly, their argument is that as large-scale industrialised societies get richer the vast majority of their populations will have incomes and assets large enough to satisfy their own social welfare needs in the private market without help from the State. They should have the right and the freedom to decide their own individual resource preferences and priorities and to buy from the private market their own preferred quantities of medical care, education, social security, housing and other services.

Unlike their distinguished predecessors in the nineteenth century, these economic analysts and politicians do not now condemn such instruments of social policy (in the form of social services) as politically irrelevant or mistaken in the past. They were needed then as temporary, *ad hoc* political mechanisms to ameliorate and reduce social conflict; to protect the rights of property, and to avoid resort to violence by the dispossessed and the deprived. This contemporary redefinition of the past role of social policy thus represents it as a form of social control; as a temporary short-term process of State intervention to buttress and legitimate industrial capitalism during its early, faltering but formative years of growth. We are now told that those who in the past were critical of State intervention in the guise of free social services were misguided and short-sighted. The Bourbons of today disavow the Bourbons of yesterday. The times, the concepts, the working classes, and the market have all changed. They have been changed by affluence, by technology, and by the development of more sophisticated, anonymous and flexible mechanisms of the market to meet social needs, to enlarge the freedom of consumer choice, and to provide not only more but better quality medical care, education, social security and housing.

In abbreviated form, these are some of the theories of private social policy and consumer choice now being advanced in Britain and other countries. Like other conceptions of social policy presented in large and all embracing terms, these theories make a number of basic assumptions about the working of the market, about the nature of social needs, and about the future social and economic characteristics of our societies. These assumptions require examination. (See, for example, D. S. Lees, " Health Through Choice " in R. Harris, *Freedom or free-for-all* ? Hobart papers vol 3, The Institute of Economic Affairs, 1965 and E. G. West, *Education and the State*, The Institute of Economics Affairs, 1965). But I cannot, however, discuss them all in as much detail as I would like in this pamphlet. I propose, therefore, to make more explicit four important assumptions and, in respect of each, to raise some questions and add some comments.

THE ECONOMIC GROWTH SOLUTION

Assumption no 1—That economic growth without the intervention of comprehensive and deliberately redistributive social policies can, by itself alone, solve the problem of poverty.

None of the evidence for Britain and the United States over the past twenty years during which the average standard of living in real terms rose by fifty per cent or more supports this assumption. The most recent evidence for Britain has been examined by Professors Abel-Smith and Townsend in their study *The poor and the poorest* (Occasional papers on social administration, no 17, Bell and sons, 1965). Had private markets in education, medical care and social security been substituted for public policies during the past twenty years of economic growth their conclusions, in both absolute and relative terms, as to the extent of poverty in Britain today would, I suggest, have been even more striking.

economic growth and poverty in the United States

For the United States the evidence is no less conclusive and can be found in the recent studies of Orshansky, Brady, S. M. Miller and Rein, Moynihan, Schorr, Herman Miller and Richard Elman whose book *The poorhouse state: The American way of life on public assistance* (Pantheon Books, New York, 1966) provides a grim picture of degradation in the richest country the world has ever known.

Yet, in 1951, the first chairman of the Council of Economic Advisors under the Eisenhower administration said, before his appointment to the Council " . . . the transformation in the distribution of our national income . . . may already be counted as one of the great social revolutions in history." (Quoted in H. T. Miller " Is the income gap closed ? ' No ' ? " *New York Times Magazine,* 11 November 1962)

Economic growth spelt progress; an evolutionary and inevitable faith that social growth would accompany economic growth. Automatically, therefore, poverty would gracefully succumb to the diffusion of the choices of private market abundance. All this heralded, as Daniel Bell and others were later to argue, the end of ideological conflict. (D. Bell, *The end of ideology: on the exhaustion of political ideas in the fifties,* New York, Collier Books, 1961)

One is led to wonder what liberal economists would have said fifteen to twenty years ago had they had foreknowledge of the growth in American wealth and had they then been asked to comment on the following facts for the year 1966 : that one American child in four would be regarded as living in poverty and that three elderly persons in ten would also be living in poverty (M. Orshansky in *Social security bulletin,* July 1963, January 1965 and July 1965, Social security administration, US department of health, education and welfare); that the United States would be moving towards a more unequal distribution of income, wealth and command-over-resources (D. S. Brady, *Age and the income distribution,* Research report no 8, Social security administration, department of health, education, and welfare, 1965. For other evidence of recent trends see S. M. Miller and M. Rein, "Poverty, inequality and policy" in H. S. Becker (ed), *Social problems,* John Wiley and Son, New York); that many grey areas would have become ghettoes (see D. R. Hunter, *The slums: challenge and response,* New York, Glencoe Free Press, 1964; H. Gans, *The Urban Villagers.* New York, Glencoe Free Press, 1962; K. E. Taeuber, *Scientific American,* 1965, vol 213, no 2; and K. E. and F. Alma Taeuber, *Negroes in cities: residential segregation and neighbourhood change,* Chicago, Aldine, 1965); that a nationwide civil rights' challenge of explosive magnitude would have to be faced—a challenge for freedom of choice, for the right to work, for a non-rat infested home, for medical care and against stigma (*The Negro family: the case for national action,* Office of policy planning and Research, us Department of Labour, 1965); that, as a nation, the United States would be seriously short of doctors, scientists, teachers, social workers, nurses, welfare aids and professional workers in almost all categories of personal service; and that American agencies would be deliberately recruiting and organising the import of doctors, nurses and other categories of human capital from less affluent nations of the world.

shortage of doctors in Britain

Britain, we should remember, is also relying heavily on the skills of doctors from poorer countries—due in part to the belief less than five to ten years ago among Conservative Ministers and leaders of the medical profession that we were in danger of training too many doctors. And, we should add, the belief among liberal economists and sections of the medical profession that Britain was spending too much on the Health Service which was in danger of bankrupting the nation.

Seven of the eleven-man committee which drew up the Ministry of Health and Department of Health for Scotland's *Report of the Committee to consider the future numbers of medical practitioners and the appropriate intake of medical students* (hmso, 1957), were eminent members of the medical profession and the chairman was an ex-Minister of Health, Sir Henry Willink. In May 1962 a special committee set up by the British Medical Association to consider recruitment to the medical profession concluded in its report that in spite of certain obvious indications of a shortage of doctors it was not prepared to commit itself on the need for more medical students. (*The Times,* 11 May 1962) Dr. R. G. Gibson, chairman of this committee (and now Chairman of the Council), said two months later that the profession had recently experienced a " glut of doctors. At present there seemed to be a shortage, but care must be taken not to create unemployment in the profession a few years from now." (*British medical journal,* supplement, ii, 26, 28 July 1962).

Guilty as we have been and are in our treatment of doctors from overseas, at least it cannot be said that we are deliberately organising recruitment campaigns in India, Pakistan and other developing countries.

THE PRIVATE MARKETS SOLUTION

Assumption no 2: That private markets in welfare can solve the problem of discrimination and stigma.

This assumption takes us to the centre of all speculations about choice in welfare and the conflict between universalist social services and selective means-tested systems for the poor. It is basically the problem of stigma or "spoiled identity" in Goffman's phrase (E. Goffman, *Stigma: notes on the management of spoiled identity*, Prentice Hall, NJ 1963); of felt and experienced discrimination and disapproval on grounds of poverty, ethnic group, class, mental fitness and other criteria of "bad risks" in all the complex processes of selection-rejection in our societies.

How does the private market in education, social security, industrial injuries insurance, rehabilitation, mental health services and medical care, operating on the basis of ability to pay and profitability, treat poor minority groups? All the evidence, particularly from the United States and Canada, suggests that they are categorised as "bad risks," treated as second class consumers, and excluded from the middle-class world of welfare. If they are excluded because they cannot pay or are likely to have above-average needs—and are offered second-class standards in a refurbished public assistance or panel system—who can blame them if they come to think that they have been discriminated against on grounds of colour and other criteria of rejection? Civil rights legislation in Britain to police the commercial insurance companies, the British United Provident Association, and the BMA's Independent Medical Services Ltd. would be a poor and ineffective substitute for the National Health Service.

Already there is evidence from recently established independent fee-paying medical practices that the "bad risks" are being excluded, and that the chronic sick are being advised to stay (if they can) with the National Health Service. (S. Mencher, *Private practice and the National Health Service*, pp 130-6, to be published). They are not offered the choice though they may be able to pay. In point of fact, their ability to choose a local doctor under the Health Service is being narrowed. This is a consequence, I suppose, of what Mr. Arthur Seldon of the Institute of Economic Affairs in his most recent essay on "choice in welfare" describes as "a new stirring in medical insurance and a new class of doctors with a grain of entrepreneurial determination to supplement or abandon the NHS and to find salvation in the market." (" Which way to welfare," *Lloyds Bank Review,* October 1966).

The essential issue here of discrimination is not the problem of choice in private welfare markets for the upper and middle classes but how to channel proportionately more economic and social resources to aid the poor, the handicapped, the educationally deprived and other minority groups, and to compensate them for bearing part of the costs of other people's progress. We cannot now, just because we are getting richer, disengage ourselves from the fundamental challenge of distributing social rights without stigma; too many unfulfilled expectations have been created, and we can no longer fall back on the *rationale* that our economies are too poor to avoid hurting people. Nor can we solve the problems of discrimination and stigma by re-creating poor law or panel systems of welfare in the belief that we should thereby be able to concentrate state help on those whose needs are greatest. Separate state systems for the poor, operating in the context of powerful private welfare markets, tend to become poor standard systems. Insofar as they are able to recruit at all for education, medical care and other services, they tend to recruit the worst rather than the best teachers, doctors, nurses, administrators and other categories of staff upon whom the quality of service so much depends. And if the quality of personal service is low, there will be less freedom of choice and more felt discrimination.

DO PRIVATE MARKETS OFFER MORE CHOICE ?

Assumption no 3: That private markets in welfare would offer consumers more choice.

As I have said, the growth of private markets in medical care, education and other welfare services, based on ability to pay and not on criteria of need, has the effects of limiting and narrowing choice for those who depend on or who prefer to use the public services.

But let us be more specific, remembering that the essential question is: *whose* freedom of choice. Let us consider this question of choice in the one field— private pension schemes—where the insurance market already operates to a substantial extent and where the philosophy of " free pensions for free men " holds sway. (A. Seldon, *Pensions in a free society,* Institute of Economic Affairs, 1957). It is, for example, maintained by the insurance industry that private schemes " are arrangements made voluntarily by individual employers with their own workers." (Life Offices' Association, *The pension problem: a statement of principle and a review of the Labour Party's proposals,* 1957, p3); that they are tailor-made and shaped to meet individual (consumer) requirements. This is, *pas excellence,* the model of consumer choice in the private welfare market, that exists today.

What are the facts ? For the vast majority of workers covered by such private schemes there is no choice. Private schemes are compulsory. Workers are not offered the choice of deferred pay or higher wages; funded schemes or pay-as-you-go schemes. They are not asked to choose between contributory or non-contributory schemes; between flat-rate systems or earnings related systems. Despite consumer evidence of a widespread wish for the provision of widows' benefits, employees are not asked to choose. There is virtually no consultation with employees or their representatives. They have no control whatsoever over the investment of funds in the hands of private insurance companies which now total some £2,500 millions (W. G. Nursaw, *Principles of pension fund investment,* p19, 1966) And, most important of all, they are rarely offered on redundancy or if they freely wish to change their jobs the choice of full preservation of pension rights. (See Report of a committee of the National Joint Advisory Council, *Preservation of pension rights,* Ministry of Labour, HMSO, 1966; the Government Actuary, *Occupational pension schemes: a new survey,* HMSO, 1966, and two forthcoming studies by T. A. Lynes, *Pensions and democracy, and Pensions in France,* occasional papers in social administration).

preservation of pension rights

These issues of transferability and the full preservation of pension rights underline strongly the urgency and importance of the Government's current review of social security. We have now been talking for over ten years about the need for freedom of industrial movement, full transferability, and adequate. value-protected pensions as " of right " in old age; it is time that the Government's proposals were made known.

But they cannot now help with the immediate problem of the redundant workers in the Midlands and other parts of the country. Have these workers forfeited their full occupational pension expectations ? What choices have been concretely offered to them by the private pension market ? I have seen no statements or surveys or reports from the insurance industry or from the Institute of Economic Affairs. Surely, here was a situation in which one might have expected the protagonists of private welfare markets to have assembled the facts, and to have demonstrated the superiority of practice as well as theory in the matter of consumer choice. But it looks as though they failed in 1966 as they failed in 1956 when the British Motor Corporation announced on the 27 June that 6,000 employees would be sacked on the 29 June. (H. R. Kahn, *Repercussions of redundancy,* Allen and Unwin, 1965) They were not offered the choice of full preservation of accrued-pension rights.

SHOULD MEDICAL CARE BE BOUGHT ?

Assumption no 4: That social services in kind, particularly medical care, have no characteristics which differentiate them from goods in the private market.

I propose to consider this last assumption in relation to medical care, and to pursue a little more intensively some of the central issues which I raised in "Ethics and economics of medical care" (*Medical care,* vol 1, no 1, 1963, p16. See also criticisms of this article by Professor Lees, Professor Jewkes and others in *Medical care,.* vol 1, no 4, 1963, pp 234-44, and D. S. Lees, "Health through choice" in *Freedom or free-for-all?* (Ed R. Harris), Hobart Papers vol 3, the Institute of Economic Affairs, 1965). This article was written in response to the thesis advanced by certain "liberal" economists in Britain and the United States who, after applying neo-classical economic theory to Western-type systems of medical care, concluded that "medical care would appear to have no characteristics which differentiate it sharply from other goods in the market." (D. S. Lees, *ibid,* pp 37-9 and 86-7). It should, therefore, be treated as a personal consumption good indistinguishable in principle from other goods. Consequently, and in terms of political action, private markets in medical care should be substituted for public markets. In support of this conclusion it is argued that the "delicate, anonymous, continuous and pervasive" mechanism of the private market (D. S. Lees, *ibid,* p64) not only makes more consumer choice possible but provides better services for a more discriminating public. Choice stimulates discrimination which, in turn, enlarges choice.

This thesis is usually presented as applying universally and in terms of the past as well as the present. It is presumed to apply to contemporary India and Tanzania as well as nineteenth-century Britain. It is, therefore, as a theoretical construct "culture free." It is also said to be value free. Medical care is a utility and all utilities are good things. But as we cannot measure the satisfactions of utilities— or compare individual satisfactions derived from different utilities—we should rely on "revealed preferences." Observable market behaviour will show what an individual chooses. Preference is what individuals prefer; no collective value judgment is consequently said to be involved.

In applying this body of doctrine to medical care we have to consider a large number of characteristics (or factors) which may or may not be said to differentiate

medical care from personal consumption goods in the market. I want to concentrate discussion on two of these factors, chiefly because I believe that one of them
is central to the whole debate about medical care, and because both of them tend
to be either ignored or treated superficially by most writers on the subject. Broadly,
they centre around the problems of uncertainty and unpredictability in medical
care and, secondly, the difficulty, in theory as well as in practice, of treating
medical care as a conceptual entity.

Consider first the problems of uncertainty which confront the consumer of medical
care. Then contrast them with the problems of the consumer of, say, cars; there
is clearly a risk to life in both situations if wrong choices are made. It is argued,
for example, by Professor Lees and others that the market for consumer durables
is affected both by unpredictability of personal demand and consumer ignorance
about needs. (D. S. Lees, *ibid*, p87). The more significant differentiating characteristics in the area of medical care would appear to be (though this is by no means
an exhaustive list) :

1. Many consumers do not desire medical care.

2. Many consumers do not know they need medical care.

3. Consumers who want medical care do not know in advance how much
medical care they need and what it will cost.

4. Consumers do not know and can rarely estimate in advance what particular
categories of medical care they are purchasing (such as surgical procedures, diag-
nostic tests, drugs, and so on).

5. Consumers can seldom learn from experience of previous episodes of medical
care consumption (not only do illnesses, or " needs," vary greatly but utility vari-
ability in medical care is generally far greater than is the case with consumer
durables).

6. Most consumers cannot assess the value of medical care (before, during or after
consumption) as an independent variable. They cannot be sure, therefore, whether
they have received " good " or " bad " medical care. Moreover, the time-scale
needed for assessment may be the total life duration.

7. Most consumers of medical care enter the doctor-patient relationship on an
unequal basis; they believe that the doctor or surgeon knows best. Unlike market
relationships in the case of consumer durables, they know that this special in-

equality in knowledge and techniques cannot for all practical purposes be reversed.

8. Medical care can seldom be returned to the seller, exchanged for durable goods or discarded. For many people the consequences of consuming medical care are irreversible.

9. Medical care knowledge is not at present a marketable advertised commodity. Nor can consumers exchange comparable valid information about the consumption of " good " or " bad " medical care.

10. Consumers of medical care experience greater difficulties in changing their minds in the course of consuming care than do consumers of durable goods.

11. Consumers of medical care may, knowingly or unknowingly, take part in or be the subject of research, teaching and controlled experiments which may affect the outcome.

12. The concept of " normal " or " average " economic behaviour on the part of adult consumers, built into private enterprise medical care models, cannot be applied automatically to the mentally ill, the mentally retarded, the seriously disabled and other categories of consumer-patients.

13. Similarly, this concept of " normal " behaviour cannot be applied automatically to immigrant populations or peoples with non-Western cultures and different beliefs and value systems.

These thirteen characteristics are indicative of the many subtle aspects of uncertainty and unpredictability which pervade modern medical care systems. " I hold " wrote Professor K. J. Arrow in an article entitled " Uncertainty and the welfare economics of medical care " in the *American economic review* (vol LIII, no 5, December 1963) " that virtually all the special features of this (medical care) industry, in fact, stem from the prevalence of uncertainty."

To grasp fully the significance of these differentiating characteristics, each one of them should be contrasted with the situation of the consumer of cars or other consumption goods; an exercise which I cheerfully leave to the reader.

I turn now to my second set of questions. Many economists who attempt to apply theories and construct models in this particular area conduct their analyses on the assumption that " medical care " is (or can be treated as) an entity. Historically, perhaps this may once have been marginally valid when it consisted almost wholly of the personal doctor-patient relationship. Medical cure, we would now say, was more a matter fifty years ago of spontaneous biological response or random chance.

Science, technology and economic growth have now, however, transformed medical care into a group process : a matter of the organised application of an immense range of specialised skills, techniques, resources and systems. If. therefore, we now wish to examine medical care from the standpoint of economic theory we need to break down this vague and generalised concept " medical care " into precise and distinctive components.

To illustrate the importance of doing so let us consider one example; probably one of the more critical components in curative medicine today, namely, the procurement, processing, matching, distribution, financing and transfusion of whole human blood. Is human blood a consumption good ?

With the data now available relating to different blood procurement programs in various countries, organised on private market principles and community welfare principles, it is now possible to consider these economic theories relating to choice and revealed preferences in respect of this particular component of medical care. Consider, first, the thesis that the " delicate mechanism " of the market works better if left by government to get on with the job: that it is more efficient; provides higher quality services; by allowing choice it generates more demand; and that it results in proportionately higher national expenditures on medical care than socialised systems like the National Health Service. Economists in Britain, West Germany and other countries who advance this thesis support it by drawing on American macro-economic data.

the New York blood transfusion services

It is appropriate, therefore, to examine the blood transfusion services in New York City and contrast them with the National Blood Transfusion Service in England and Wales. National statistics for the USA are fragmentary and defective in many respects. One reason is the great variety from area to area in the programs of the American Red Cross, community, hospital and commercial blood banks and services. More information is, however, available for particular cities and areas. It must not be assumed that what obtains in New York is generally applicable in the USA. For a community of some 8,000,000 people, New York uses about 330,000 pints of blood a year. (The New York Blood Center, *Progress report for* 1965, Community Blood Council of Greater New York, Inc, 1965). In England and Wales in 1965 the number of blood donations totalled approximately 1,300,000. (*Annual report of the Ministry of Health for* 1965, Cmnd 3039, 1966, table 75). It is variously guessed for the USA as a whole that some

6,000,000 pints of blood are collected annually. (American Medical Association, *Directory of blood banking and transfusion facilities and services,* Chicago)

Figures of this order indicate the indispensable and increasingly vital part played by blood transfusion services in modern medicine. The transfer of blood from one human being to another represents one of the greatest therapeutic instruments in the hands of the doctor. It has made possible the saving of life on a scale undreamt of a few decades ago and for conditions which would then have been considered hopeless. The demand for blood increases yearly in every Western country as new uses are developed ; as more radical surgical techniques are adopted which are associated with the loss of massive amounts of blood ; as road accidents continue to rise ; and with the increasingly widespread use of artificial heart-lung machines in open heart surgery (first developed in Britain in 1950) and for numerous other reasons. It is a precious commodity yet in Britain (with a wholly voluntary program of blood donations) without price. If carelessly or wrongly used it can be more lethal than many drugs. Because of the risks of transmitting the virus of infective hepatitis (homologous serum hepatitis) and other diseases the most rigorous standards are set in Britain in the selection of blood donors, and in the cross-matching, testing and transfusion of blood.

Not only is human blood potentially lethal to the recipient but it has the critical characteristic of " 21-day perishability." Its value rapidly expires. This particular characteristic presents great administrative and technical problems in the operation of blood transfusion services ; in the estimation of demand for blood of different groups ; in the organisation, planning and execution of blood donor programs ; in the technical organisation of compatibility tests and cross-matching ; and in the distribution of supplies of whole blood in the right quantities and categories, at the right times, and to the right hospitals and the right patients.

After this brief explanation of some of the important factors to bear in mind, I want now to present some information about the present situation in New York. Despite the fact that there are over 150 independent agencies handling blood in New York, some operating on a profit basis and many buying blood from so-called " professional " donors, there is an acute and chronic shortage of blood. (The New York Blood Center, *ibid,* pp 2-11). Operations are postponed daily because of the shortage. " Professional " donors from " Skid row denizens," drug addicts and others who live by selling their blood (at $10 to $25 or more a pint) are often bled more frequently than accepted international standards recommend, and far more frequently than the much higher standard set in Britain. (R. F. Norris, *et al, Transfusion,* 3 pp 202-9, 1963, and *Medical World News* 15 March 1963). There is evidence from a number of American cities in which studies have been made that something like 30 to 40 per cent of paid blood donors are unemployed and predominantly unskilled workers. In Chicago, the Blood Donor Service reported a figure of 40.6 per cent for 1965 (personal correspondence with Medical Director, July-August 1966). In 1964, the latest year available, 60 per cent of all donors bled by this Service were paid.

The shortage of blood in New York and other cities is in part due to a large amount of wasted blood (resulting from blood-hoarding by hospitals and other agencies) and to the hazardous quality of "professional" blood. In consequence, blood charges and blood bills remitted to patients are high. Some commercial blood banks in New York import blood from Tennessee, and such banks in the USA have attempted to import blood from England and Australia.

The New York Academy of Medicine reported in 1956 that the city was relying on "professional" donors to the extent of about 42 per cent for its blood supplies. (*Human blood in New York City*, (privately circulated), New York Academy of Medicine, Committee on Public Health, 1956) In 1965 the estimated figure was 55 per cent. (New York Blood Center, private communication from Dr. A. Kellner, June 1966) "Professional" donors cannot be expected to be as truthful in clinical history-taking as unpaid volunteers. Studies at the University of Chicago and elsewhere have demonstrated that the chances of the "professional" donor being a carrier of hepatitis "are essentially six times greater than those of the volunteer or family donor." (J. Garrott Allen and W. A. Sayman, JAMA, 180: 1079, 1962) The virus cannot be detected in the laboratory. The patient is the test. The doctor is thus faced with the choice of withholding blood or transfusing blood which may have been obtained from a "professional" donor—if he knows, which he rarely does, the source of the blood.

the contrasting situation in Britain

In Britain, the situation is incomparably different. There is no shortage of blood. It is freely donated by the community for the community. It is a free gift from the healthy to the sick irrespective of income, class, ethnic group, religion, private patient or public patient. Since the National Health Service was established the quantity of blood issued to hospitals has risen by 265 per cent. (*Annual Reports of the Ministry of Health*)

The question I have raised whether human blood is a trading commodity, a market good like aspirins or cars, or a service rendered by the community for the community, is no idle academic question asked in a philosophical mood. In the last few years it has become in the USA a battle ground for lawyers and economists. The costs incurred by respondents in debating this question in one case alone (involving the Federal Trade Commission and a blood bank in Kansas City) have amounted to $250,000 (*Transfusion*, 5, 2 : 207, March-April 1963) Dr. R. L. Mainwaring, President-elect in 1964 of the American Association of Blood Banks, has said that if blood is legally designated as a commodity (thus endorsing commercial practise) "Hospital insurance rates would go sky high. The laboratory director would not be able to rely on anyone else to screen his blood; he would have to do it himself. And, even with perfect cross-matches he could expect that one out of every 200 pints he provided would carry hepatitis virus." (*Transfusion*, 4 : 68, 1964)

less choice for the consumer

There is much more that I could say (and shall hope to say elsewhere) on these complex issues. But I find no support here for the model of choice in the private market; on criteria of efficiency, of efficacy, of quality, or of safety. No consumer can estimate, in advance, the nature of these and other hazards; few, in any event, will know that they are to be the recipient of someone else's blood. In this private market in New York and other American cities the consumer is not sovereign. He has less choice; he is simultaneously exposed to greater hazards; he pays a far higher price for a more hazardous service; he pays, in addition, for all the waste in the system; and he further pays for an immense and swollen bureaucracy required to administer a complex banking system of credits, deposits, charges, transfers and so forth. Above all, it is a system which neglects and punishes the indigent, the coloured, the dispossessed and the deviant.

The characteristics of uncertainty and unpredictability are the dominating ones in this particular component of medical care. They are the product of scientific advances accentuated, as this study shows, by the application of inapplicable economic theories to the procurement and distribution of human blood.

I draw one other conclusion from this discussion. Socialism is about community as well as equality. It is about what we contribute without price to the community and how we act and live as socialists—and not just about how we debate socialism.

poverty, socialism, and labour in power

Peter Townsend

It will be one of the supreme paradoxes of history if social inequalities become wider instead of narrower and poverty more widespread during the term in office of the present Labour Government. Yet the likelihood of this happening is far from remote. Here is a political movement whose egalitarian ideals were nurtured by the degradations which millions of men, women and children endured during the nineteenth century in mines, factories and slums. These ideals are vigorously expressed today on the shop floor, within the trade unions, at ward meetings and at party conferences. Men have come to regard the achievement of equality as the essence of socialism. Much that is important and indeed noble in the search for a humane social order, unselfishness, partnership, solidarity, fair shares, common responsibility and, above all, the elimination of poverty is crystallised in the concept. This central motivation carried the Labour Party to power in 1945 and played a big part in the victories of 1964 and 1966.

Given the history and ideals of the Labour Movement how is it possible to conceive, therefore, that the problems of poverty and inequality might be growing? Brian Abel-Smith has discussed already the shortcomings of forward planning and has shown in terms of this country's recent experience and developments in other industrial countries that the social services are being starved of resources. (*Labour's Social Plans,* Fabian tract 369) Richard Titmuss has shown that the private market is incapable of solving the problems of poverty, discrimination and unequal access to education, social security and medical care. (*Choice and "The Welfare State,"* Fabian tract 370) I shall argue first that the problem of poverty in modern society is different from conventional or traditional interpretations, that it is big and is growing. It therefore demands more comprehensive action to solve than might be supposed if the traditional interpretation were followed. Second I shall argue that even by conventional standards the extent of poverty in Britain has been and is underestimated and, third, that the Labour Government has as yet done little to meet such poverty. Finally, I shall try to suggest the kind of measures which have to be given priority for socialist objectives to be reached.

different conceptions of poverty

There are many different conceptions of poverty. The individual may feel he is poor, in relation to the people around him, the job he is expected to perform or his past experience. Collective or conventional views tend to be reflected in the minimum standards of social security benefit which are adopted in different countries. (see: Brian Abel-Smith and Peter Townsend, *The poor and the poorest,* Bell, 1965, O. Ornati, *Poverty amid affluence.* The twentieth century fund, New York, 1966, S, M. Miller and M. Rein, " Poverty, inequality and policy " *Social problems* (ed H. S. Becker) John Wiley, New York—forthcoming) Those with less income than the minimum rates of benefit are regarded as in poverty.

Within a single country different organisations may hold conflicting views. For example, local authorities in Britain vary widely in the means tests they apply in educational, home help and housing services. A single organisation too, may apply different conceptions simultaneously. The Government's definition of subsistence varies from around £50 a week for class A employees working temporarily in Paris, £21 a week for employees or consultants on official business in this country to around £5 10s a week (including average rent) for citizens on national assistance.

Is there an objective or scientific approach ? Historically much has been made of a basic " subsistence " level—meaning, in its restricted sense, the minimum resources needed by a man or a family to get enough to eat and maintain physical health. The trouble with this approach is that contrary to common supposition nutritional needs cannot be strictly defined and to a large extent are relative to the social and occupational conditions in which they arise. If men are expected to expend their energies in steelworks or mines rather than look after a herd of camels they need more to eat and drink. But practically no scientific study has been made of variations of diet according to both social and occupational environment. Whether those in sedentary occupations, like clerks, pass their evenings and weekends in violent physical exercise—playing football and ballroom dancing— while the miners have their feet up in front of a television set is unknown. Second, even in agricultural societies there are psychological and social needs as basic as nutritional or physical needs which can be met only by the expenditure of resources in money or kind. Third, in industrial societies the individual and the family plainly have to meet new obligations which are thrust upon them—whether by local housing or education authorities, the state, modern technology and marketing or simply changing social norms and values.

A vivid example of the insistence of society that individuals conform to modern standards was a case in New York of an old man who was denied welfare because he refused to give up sleeping on rags in a barn. The Court's considered opinion included this gem : "Appellant also argues that he has a right to live as he pleases while being supported by public charity. One would admire his independence if he were not so dependent, but he has no right to defy the standards and conventions of civilised society while being supported at public expense." (Quoted by C. A. Reich, " The New Property," *The Yale law journal*, vol 73, no 5, April 1964).

relative poverty

Human needs arise by virtue of the kind of society to which individuals belong. We can therefore consider such needs meaningfully only in relation to various social groups and systems—ranging from households, families, local communities and national societies to, finally, international society. Any rational definition of poverty must be relative. Consequently, if it is to be applied at different points of time during periods of economic and social growth it must be upgraded, and not merely repriced.

This helps to explain inconsistencies which arise in the world today. United Nations and other experts have produced standards of subsistence for some developing countries far in excess of the resources commanded by the average wage-earner in those countries but far below the standards adopted in advanced industrial countries (for example, *Assistance to the needy in less developed areas*, Department of economic and social affairs, United Nations, New York 1956). The national income per head in India, Bolivia, the Congo and Pakistan, when translated into us dollars, is *on average* less than 100 dollars a year. The amount required by the *poor* to survive is far less. Yet the standard officially adopted in the United States below which people are described as in poverty, ranges from about 1500 dollars a year for a person living alone to about 700 dollars a head for large families (M. Orshansky, "Counting the poor : another look at the poverty line," *Social security bulletin*, vol 28, January 1965).

" subsistence standards "

There is a reluctance to accept evidence that so-called " subsistence " standards are dramatically higher in advanced industrial than in developing countries, and there is an equal reluctance at least in Britain and the United States, to accept the evidence that such standards have been or ought to be upgraded in the course of time. There are political as well as social and psychological reasons for this. The subsistence or national minimum has a hallowed history. In Britain the basic rates payable by the Supplementary Benefits Commission and Ministry of Social Security are distantly related to the levels advocated in the Beveridge Report in the war, which in turn reflected the standards used in measuring poverty by Rowntree and others before the war. Many people like to believe the national minimum has a scientific basis. First of all, when used as a measure of poverty only a minority of the population are found in fact to be exposed to this problem. Wages in industrial countries are usually enough to maintain physical efficiency. Second, if the same measure is applied in later years the proportion in poverty is found to diminish. This is very comforting for politicians. But if the standard is adjusted only for price increases the diminution is inevitable. Since real incomes in industrial countries tend to rise, the proportion of the population " left behind " is almost bound to shrink. Seebohm Rowntree liberalised the measure of poverty which he had used in York in 1899 when he undertook a second survey in 1936 and again when he undertook a third survey in 1950, but not to the same extent as real increases in wages. Partly (though not wholly) as a consequence he found fewer people in poverty—the percentage falling from 28 to 18 and then to 2 at the three dates (B. S. Rowntree and G. R. Lavers, *Poverty in the welfare state,* Longmans, 1951). Similarly, by applying its standard of subsistence, the Social Security Administration of the United States has found an encouraging reduction in poverty from 22 per cent to 18 per cent during five recent years. As the 1964 *Economic Report of the President of the United States* declared with pride (p110) " five years of prosperity and continued economic expansion have contributed significantly to reducing the number of people who live in poverty. Between 1959 and 1964, the number of persons defined as poor decreased from 38.9 million to 34.1 million." But the failure to revise the measure in accordance with wage increases and social changes largely invalidates the result.

Third, the whole concept of a national minimum invites selective, ameliorative and isolated rather than universal and reconstructional policies to relieve poverty. Social and economic reforms, it is supposed, do not have to be drastic. Providing welfare can be concentrated among the pockets or islands of the population where it is needed all will be well. The rich, the middle-income groups, the status, income and class hierarchies of society and the values and standards of many professional and voluntary associations will not be threatened. Minor adjustments alone are needed.

The subsistence standard or national minimum has an ideological rather than a scientific basis. It reflects the separatist social philosophy flowing historically from the less-eligibility principle of the English Poor Law. The income-levels of the poor, it is supposed, have to be determined differently from those of the rest of the population—as if they were a race apart. Sargant Shriver, director of the us President's War Against Poverty, has complained of the tendency in the United States for many to speak of " we the people " and " they the poor." Broadly, the poor are allowed living room on a " floor " at the bottom of the hierarchial social structure, above which they are expected to rise by their own efforts. They have to struggle for a foothold on the ladders to the more affluent levels of society, irrespective of the fact that there are places enough on neither the ladders nor the upper storeys for more than a few more of them and irrespective of the fact that chutes from the upper storeys are regularly transporting individuals and families to the nether levels.

It is only in terms of a modern version of Brueghel's Tower of Babel, as representing hierarchical society, that we can perceive the limitations of the " national minimum " approach to poverty. Each level of society may be on an escalator of socio-economic growth, and there may be machinery for slightly reducing or increasing the distance between levels. But the structure determines poverty. In relation to the resources commonly sought after and commonly acknowledged to be necessary there is a section of the population which is deprived of commanding them.

defining resources

What is the alternative approach ? Individuals and families can be defined as in poverty when they lack or fall seriously short of the resources commanded by the average members of society. This might of course be discussed at great length but two matters deserve special attention. The idea of what constitutes individual or family " resources " in modern society has to be revised. We can no longer talk about poverty only in terms of the money income coming in week by week. There are people with small incomes but substantial other resources (including assets) and vice versa. The ownership of assets can be important in maintaining living standards, especially among the middle-aged and old. There are not only assets like savings and housing, but also cars, boats and household possessions. Some people have powers to distribute the realisation of assets over time (see R. M. Titmuss, *Income distribution and social change*, Allen and Unwin, 1962). Then there are fringe benefits—such as luncheon vouchers, educational endowment, superannuation payments and travel and housing expenses. Recent estimates suggest that the cost of fringe benefits to employers is over 10 per cent of the earnings bill in Britain and still rising. (G. L. Reid and D. J. Robertson, *Fringe benefits, labour costs and social security*, Allen and Unwin, 1965) In one study fringe benefits accounted for an extra 31 per cent of the £7,000 average earnings of company managers but 11 per cent of the £1,000 average earnings of those at the foot of the salary scale (A study by Hay—MSL Management Consultants, *The Times*, 11 August 1966) For some families income in kind, such as gifts and services from relatives and neighbours, is of major importance.

Account must also be taken of current consumption of public social services and private possession of public assets, such as the use of free or subsidised housing and office-space and the possession of assets such as educational qualifications. Too readily in the past it has been supposed that universal public services have automatically conferred equality of access as well as equality of rights. The wealth dispensed by government is, as Charles Reich has argued, the new property (*op cit*) Who owns this property and how such ownership is measured are important questions. For example, more middle-class than working-class students gain University degrees at State expense. National Health Service lists and school classes tend to be larger in working-class areas.

The Newsom Report describes in particular the disadvantages of the schools in slum areas. Seventy-nine per cent of them, compared with 40 per cent of secondary modern schools generally, are in buildings which are seriously inadequate. The turnover of staff is much higher. Fewer pupils stay on an extra term or two beyond the minimum leaving age and fewer belong to school clubs and societies. (A report of the Central Advisory Council for Education (England) *Half our future*, HMSO, 1963).

Many of the poorest people seem not to qualify for subsidised Council housing or are obliged to leave it for far worse and usually more costly privately rented housing. The Milner Holland Committee on Housing in Greater London has described the rigidities in housing supply and the difficulties of various classes of tenants. " The people who suffer most from housing stress are those with the lowest incomes, those with average incomes and large families, and many of the newcomers to London." (*Report of the Committee on Housing in Greater London*, Cmnd 2605, HMSO, March 1965, p91; see also pp127-131) In France " the poorest families cannot get into the low-rent flats for letting which in theory are designed for them. . . . In the present state of the law, low-income families are therefore inexorably forced into slum neighbourhoods, squalid furnished accommodation or ' the grey areas ' on the outskirts of the town." When slums are torn down " the destruction of their neighbourhoods involves the destruction of a whole network of relationships and communications, drives them further from their place of work, deprives them of their accommodation with its very low rent and the last remaining amenities (running water, for example)." (M. Parodi, " France," *Low income groups and methods of dealing with their problems* OECD, Paris, 1966).

other groups without access to welfare

Other groups may not have access to welfare. Many migrants, especially from overseas, cannot qualify for years for admission to housing waiting lists. Of men who were unemployed in August 1966 nearly half did not receive unemployment benefit and half of these did not get national assistance. Some of those getting unemployment benefit did not qualify for the full rate (*Ministry of Labour Gazette*, October 1966).

Separated and divorced wives and widows may not qualify for supplementary benefits. The Supplementary Benefits Commission has powers to refuse benefit to a mother when it believes it has evidence of her living with a man. Anonymous letters are sometimes acted upon. There are individual officers who have responsibility for investigating fraudulent claims. Some mothers report instances of officers searching rooms and cupboards without permission in attempts to check whether or not there are men present or are articles of men's clothing lying around. These inquiries do not appear to be as ruthless as those in some parts of the world.

In certain areas of the United States, for example, special investigation teams pay surprise visits in the middle of the night and search the house for any sign of a man, with unnerving effects on the entire family (see Greenleigh Association, *Facts, fallacies and the future*, A study of the aid to dependent children program of Cook county, Illinois 64, 1960). All these are the kind of issues with which we will be obliged increasingly to deal.

Families vary in their command of these kinds of resources. A family may be in poverty in terms of all or only some of them. It may have low monetary income, no liquid assets, no educational capital, access only to a dilapidated hospital and an overworked general practitioner partnership; the children may go to a slum school and the home itself may be a slum. Alternatively, only some of these deprivations may apply. The distinction between total and partial poverty is one which must be made in industrial society. Both kinds of poverty are significant. This analysis also suggests that some of the people who are excluded in surveys of income and expenditure, such as children in children's homes and adults in long-stay hospitals and residential homes, may be found to be in poverty. Isolated institutions can too quickly fall behind the standards of living being attained by the population in private households. By comparison with standards of living enjoyed by people of the same age in the general community, there is evidence of the inmates of many psychiatric hospitals, hospitals for chronic disease and welfare institutions being in poverty. (J. H. Sheldon, *Report to the Birmingham Regional Hospital Board on its geriatric services*, Birmingham, RHB, 1961, K. Jones and R. Sidebotham, *Mental hospitals at work*, Routledge, 1962, P. Townsend, *The Last Refuge*, Routledge, 1962).

level of resources

The second matter which is crucial to a revised conception of poverty is the level of resources at which it is justified to begin talking of " poverty." In descending the various scales of resources it is in principle possible to establish when there are significant departures from social norms and conditions. For example, in many surveys the proportion of household expenditure devoted to food has been found to be fairly constant for middle-income groups but increases sharply below particular levels of income. The point at which the proportion changes could be treated as the point below which people may be found to be in poverty. Future research might establish other indices of exclusion from participation in particular social customs and relationships, such as inability to take holidays away from home, keep children at school, replenish stocks of clothes, have regular cooked meals and entertain guests and treat friends at home or outside the home. President Johnson's advisers have sometimes recognised the problem and have searched for formulations going beyond the traditional conception of poverty. In his message on poverty to Congress in 1964, for example, the President asked, " What does this poverty mean to those who endure it ? " First, he gave the traditional interpretation. " It means a daily struggle to secure the necessities for even a meagre existence." But he then went on, *" It means that the abundance, the comforts, the opportunities they see all around them are beyond their grasp."* (author's italics). (*The war on poverty: the Economic Opportunity Act of* 1964, US Gov printing office, Washington, 1964).

THE SCALE AND NATURE OF POVERTY

We are struggling to identify and measure these new forms of poverty. In Britain it could be argued that they began to be recognised around the mid nineteen-fifties. Earlier the Labour movement and the general public assumed that through its Welfare State policies the Attlee government had consolidated the greater social equality ushered in by the war. In the words of the Chairman of the National Food Survey Committee in his preface to the committee's 1958 annual report (*Domestic food consumption and expenditure,* HMSO, 1960) we had witnessed the " virtual elimination " of poverty.

the extent of poverty

At first the problem was thought to apply to a substantial section of the aged but to relatively few other persons in the population. In writing of the United States, where unemployment was heavy in some areas, J. K. Galbraith referred to " islands " of poverty. (*The affluent society,* chap 23, Hamish Hamilton, 1958) It was difficult in both countries to believe that despite new legislation and rising prosperity there remained large-scale hardship. Yet a gradually accumulating literature on the aged, widows, the sick and the unemployed in Britain, and a few income studies in the United States led to a partial realisation of the size of the problem. (See P. Marris, *Widows and their families,* Routledge, 1958, L. A. Shaw and M. Bowerbank, " Living on a state-maintained income, I and II," *Case Conference,* March and April 1958). Finally a quantitative measure was obtained of what at least was conventionally regarded as " poverty." In the United States 38 million people or 22 per cent were found to have incomes below those thought necessary to secure a reasonable minimum diet. (M. Orshansky, *op cit*). In Britain the proportion of " subsistence " poverty was found to be smaller but still substantial. An analysis of income data collected for 1960 by the Ministry of Labour suggested that between seven and eight million persons, or around 14 per cent, were living below a specially defined " national assistance " standard, i.e., a standard incorporating the basic national assistance rates and average rent plus a margin, 40 per cent, to cover income which was disregarded by the National Assistance Board and small additions commonly made at the Board's discretion (B. Abel-Smith and P. Town-send, *op cit*) The American standard is in real terms much higher than the British " poverty line " but judged in relation to average earnings is about equal. Moreover, more of the poor in the United States than in Britain are markedly below the line. The studies in both countries revealed the unpalatable fact that hardship existed among a substantial number of families of wage-earners.

Not only are the numbers of the poor large. They are almost certainly growing. For some years it has been generally recognised that " on the whole . . . the economic inequalities between developed and underdeveloped countries have been increasing." (G. Myrdal, *Economic theory and underdeveloped regions*, p6, Methuen, 1963) The possibility that a similar process may be occurring *within* the developed countries is just beginning to dawn. In many of them there have been relative increases in some groups in the population who have been at an economic disadvantage in the years since the war. Thus, there has been a shift in structure of the adult population towards the older age-groups; a revival of the birth-rate together with an increase in the number of families with four or more children; and small increases in the numbers of chronic sick, disabled and handicapped among the middle and older age-groups. Certain forms of dependency may in fact increase in advanced societies. Secondly, the differential development of state and private welfare schemes has reinforced social divisions. The growth of occupa-tional sick pay and superannuation schemes has made a mockery of the minimum benefits of national insurance schemes. The real value of family allowances has been eroded while that of children's tax allowances has increased. The teaching and facilities in many slum-area schools has remained abysmal while that in many suburban and housing-estate schools has greatly improved. There is inequality within the state sector as well as between the public and private sectors. Thirdly, it is possible that flagging demand for unskilled workers, together with the continuing increase in the employment of married women and the greater opportunity for cer-tain workers to maintain two jobs has held down the wage-rates of some male employees and thrown a number into premature retirement. These are some of the critical factors.

the character of the problem

What therefore was the problem faced by the Labour Party when it achieved power in October 1964 ? Among those in poverty are the following :

1. Families in which the head is in full-time work but has either a relatively low wage or several children or both (the estimated number of persons living below a national assistance standard, including rent and a margin of 40 per cent extra to allow for income disregards and discretionary additions, (B. Abel-Smith and

P. Townsend, *op cit*) is three million, of whom rather less than a million have incomes below the basic national assistance rates, including average rent paid).

2.   Persons of pensionable age, whether living alone, as married couples or with others in the household (the estimated number living below a national assistance standard is about $2\frac{1}{2}$ million, of whom about 850,000 have incomes of less than the basic national assistance rates, including average payment for rent).

3.   Families composed of a mother and dependent children but no father (estimated number of persons below the standard being around $\frac{3}{4}$ million, of whom possibly as many as 300,000 have incomes of less than the basic national assistance rates).

4.   Families in which one parent, not necessarily the head or the father of a family, is disabled or has been sick for three months or more (estimated number of persons living below the standard being about $\frac{3}{4}$ million including up to $\frac{1}{4}$ million with incomes of less than the basic national assistance rates).

5.   Families with a father who is unemployed (estimated number of persons living below the standard being at least $\frac{1}{2}$ million at the present time, of whom at least $\frac{1}{4}$ million have incomes of less than the basic national assistance rates).

Although these groups are not exhaustive they are the principal ones and are discussed below.

wage earner families

Too little is yet known about living standards in these families. The Ministry of Social Security's report on a survey of households with children is eagerly awaited. A pilot study of families in London with five or more children has shown that nearly a quarter have incomes below the basic national assistance rates and another sixth only up to 20 per cent more than these rates. (Hilary Land, " Provision for large families," *New Society*, 24 November 1966) The man's wage is below the total that would be allowed under the national assistance or what is now the supplementary benefits scheme.   Some families' incomes do not reach the total even when the wife takes paid employment to supplement her husband's inadequate wage.

.The problem is by no means confined to large families.   The latest work of a research team at the University of Essex and the London School of Economics, on a national survey of poverty financed by the Joseph Rowntree Memorial Trust, suggests that a significant minority of wage-earner households with two or three children—perhaps 10 per cent—fall below national assistance, or supplementary benefit, levels. It also suggests that a disproportionately large proportion of men with low wages are disabled or have histories of ill-health and disability. In October 1960, when the average wage was £14 3s, a survey of manual earnings in selected manufacturing industries carried out by the Ministry of Labour showed that as many as 10 per cent of men aged 21 and over were receiving less than £10 a week. About 30 per cent had earnings of less than 80 per cent of the average. (*Ministry of Labour Gazette*, April and June 1961) The survey had severe limitations. It did not cover earnings in agriculture, transport, docks and mining, for example, did not extend to clerical, technical and supervisory staff and referred to only 73 per cent of the total number of manual workers employed in the selected industries. None the less the survey was the most comprehensive yet carried out by the Ministry.

family expenditure

A recent report of the Family Expenditure Survey allows us to go further— though the precision of the data is still uncertain. As with preceding income and expenditure surveys the response rate was low and it is possible that fewer of those with low earnings than with average or high earnings responded. An analysis of the earnings of male employees aged 21 and over who were covered by the 1965 Survey showed that 8 per cent, representing more than a million, were earning under £12 per week, or less than 60 per cent of the average earnings, which were then nearly £20. (By April 1966 average earnings had risen to £20 5s, *Ministry of Labour Gazette*, October 1966) About 41 per cent, or 6 million, had earnings of less than 80 per cent of the average. Employees in manufacturing industry tended to earn rather more. Few of them had earnings of less than 80 per cent of the average (the figure for *manual* workers being 22 per cent, compared with 30 per cent in the 1960 special inquiry). The report shows that there are substantial proportions of manual workers in the extractive and service industries earning considerably less than the average, and also that there are some non-manual workers with very low earnings (Ministry of Labour, *Family expenditure survey, report for* 1965, pp 3-4, HMSO, 1966).

Without further information about the regularity of earnings, household composition and other sources of household income it is difficult to judge the meaning of these earnings data. Some people with low earnings live in households where there are other earners. The number of wives in paid employment has been rising steadily since the war and is now around 4½ millions. Despite this increase the number of households with more than one earner has been falling. At the 1961 Census 42 per cent of all households in England and Wales had more than one earner, and 13 per cent three or more earners. This compares with 46 per cent and 15 per cent respectively at the 1951 Census. The increase in married women in paid employment seems to be more than balanced by the increase in numbers of " retirement " households, the falling number of composite households and more adolescents in households who stay on at school.

retired persons

A series of local and national studies allows us to be fairly precise about the income levels of the aged. The incomes of a majority are low. In 1962 nearly 1¾ million men and women aged 65 and over (or about half of all single and widowed persons) had total incomes of less than £4 a week, and 400,000 couples (or just under a quarter of all couples) less than £6 a week. They accounted for well over half the total of nearly 6 million persons of this age and corresponded roughly with those whose incomes derived wholly from the State together with those who had no more than £1 a week in addition to State benefits. The median income of the retired is about half that of younger persons in the population who have no dependants. (P. Townsend and D. Wedderburn, with S. Korte and S. Benson, *The aged in the welfare state,* Occasional papers on social administration, no 14, Bell, 1965).

There is another way of expressing the relatively low incomes of the majority of the elderly. A quarter of retirement pensioners, or around 1½ million, receive national assistance but at least another ¾ million do not receive assistance and yet would seem to qualify for it. A further million do not qualify but are only marginally better off. Social scientists who made cautious estimates of these numbers in the nineteen-fifties were derided by Government Ministers and by the Chairman of the National Assistance Board and yet eventually vindicated (for example D. Cole Wedderburn with J. Utting, *The economic circumstances of old people,* occasional papers on social administration, no 4, 1962). The Allen Committee of Inquiry into the Impact of Rates on Households and the Ministry of Pensions survey-report on retirement pensioners both concluded that between half a million and a million retirement pensioners were eligible for national assistance and were not receiving it. The Allen Committee estimated that there were 800,000 *households* with retired heads (containing over a million retired persons) who were " apparently eligible for national assistance but not getting it." Even allowing for some understatement of incomes they concluded that about half a million households were eligible. (*Report of the committee of inquiry into the impact of rates on households,* p117, Cmnd 2582, HMSO, 1965) The Ministry's study showed that 34 per cent of widowed and unmarried female retirement pensioners were receiving national assistance, that another 21 per cent were provisionally entitled to it and that only 19 per cent had a net available income exceeding needs (as defined by the national assistance scale rates) by £1 a week or more. The corresponding figures for widowed and unmarried male pensioners are 22, 13 and 33; and for married pensioners 18, 11 and 50. (Ministry of Pensions and National Insurance, *Financial and other circumstances of retirement pensioners*, pp 20 and 83-4, HMSO, 1966).

Another common assumption must also be questioned. Occupational pensions add significantly to the incomes of only a minority of the retired—two thirds of whom, it should be noted, are women. Forty-eight per cent of men, 24 per cent of women on their own insurance and 11 per cent of widows draw such pensions. A third of the men, a quarter of the women and a half of the widows receive less than 30 shillings a week. Moreover, three-quarters of those with pensions from the private sector have not received an increase since they first started getting them. (*ibid*, pp 154-163).

fatherless families

The Census of 1961 shows that for England and Wales there were approximately 400,000 families in which there were dependent children under 16 years of age but only one parent, usually the mother—accounting for a million persons, including 600,000 children. About 6 per cent of all children are in such families and the Family Expenditure Survey shows that their incomes are low. For example, in 1953-4 8 per cent of all children in Britain were in households living below a defined national assistance standard but as many as 36 per cent of children in households consisting of one woman and two or more children were living at this standard. (B. Abel-Smith and P. Townsend, *op cit*, p32) To take another index of comparison, in 1953-4 the average expenditure of households consisting of a woman and two or more children was 160 shillings; whereas the average expenditure of a household containing a man, woman and one child was 240 shillings, as much as 50 per cent more. (Ministry of Labour, *Family expenditure survey*, Report for 1953-4, London, HMSO, 1957). A pilot study by Dennis Marsden at the University of Essex reveals that compared with widows, separated and divorced wives with children tend to be poorer and unsupported mothers of illegitimate children are poorest of all. Not only do they feel stigmatised socially; their incomes are more insecure and irregular, based as they are on national assistance and court orders; they do not receive state benefits as of right and stringent earnings rules are applied when they receive assistance. (D. Marsden, *Fatherless families in a northern and a south eastern area of England*, forthcoming).

The 1965 annual report of the National Assistance Board (p27, Cmnd 3042, HMSO, 1966) shows that there are 104,000 women separated permanently from their husbands and receiving assistance of whom 50,000 have neither court orders nor out-of-court agreements. There are 43,000 with court orders, only

21,000 of whom receive maintenance regularly; of the remainder 15,000 receive no payments at all.

the sick and the disabled

During 1964-5 about 456,000 persons below pensionable age had been off work and receiving sickness benefits for three months or more. Of these as many as 310,000 had been receiving benefits for twelve months or more. (Ministry of Social Security personal communication) There were 275,00 persons receiving war disablement pensions with 30 per cent or more disablement (three-fifths of them in the 1939 war or subsequently) and another 90,000 with industrial injury disablement pensions, also with 30 per cent or more disablement. (*Report of the Ministry of Pensions and National Insurance for the year* 1965, pp 97 and 146, HMSO, 1966). Many of these were also receiving sickness benefits, but an additional 139,000 incapacitated persons received national assistance allowances only. Most of these had been incapacitated since birth or early childhood (*Report of the National Assistance Board for the year ended* 31 *December* 1965, pp 6-8, Cmnd 3042, HMSO 1966).

Although the precise numbers drawing both sickness benefit and war or industrial injury pensions are not known it seems that there are in the population at least 750,000 persons under pension age who are disabled or long-term sick. About 240,000 receive national assistance in some form and perhaps another 50,000 to 100,000 might qualify for supplementation or basic assistance. If we add dependants these figures become around 400,000 and 120,000 to 240,000.

the unemployed

In November 1966 approximately 575,000 were unemployed, of whom 160,000 had been unemployed two months or more. Altogether, probably 150,000 people have experienced 6 months unemployment during the past year. Some experience recurrent short spells of unemployment rather than long spells (R. A. Sinfield, *Unemployed in Shields*—forthcoming) The Ministry of Labour carried out a special survey of the unemployed in October 1964 and found that half of the women and 60 per cent of the men were " poor placing prospects on various personal grounds." This categorisation is highly ambiguous if not prejudicial but those on the list included many who were disabled or who had a history of ill-health. As many as 8 per cent of the women and 10 per cent of the men were registered disabled persons. In December 1965 as many as 112,000 unemployed persons received assistance. Together with their dependants they numbered 272,000 Of these about 88,000, nearly a third, were in households affected by the wage stop. (*Report of the National Assistance Board for the year ended* 31 December 1965, pp 30 and 61)

widening inequalities in Britain

The problem in 1964 was not, however, one just of scant monetary resources. At a time of growing demand for higher education how could the proportion of working class children reaching the sixth forms and going on to university be increased? Broadly speaking, inequalities of educational opportunity have not been reduced over a generation. In the 1950's only $\frac{1}{2}$ per cent of the children of unskilled and semi-skilled manual workers were reaching the universities, about the same proportion as in the late 1930s and 1940s. About $14\frac{1}{2}$ per cent of the children of professional, managerial and intermediate occupational groups were doing so, compared with 6 per cent in the 1930s and 1940s. In recent years one in every four of the non-manual middle class children entering a grammar school type course at the age of 11, but only one in every 15 to 20 of unskilled manual workers' children entering such a course have eventually gone on to a university. (A. Little and J. Westergaard, "The trend of class differentials in educational opportunity in England and Wales," *British Journal of Sociology*, 1964). We should also remember that in comparing utilisation of educational facilities there has been a rapid expansion in university courses for graduate students, the majority of whom are middle class. But of course the problem of the distribution of educational resources affects children of all ages and not just students entering university. How is it possible to steer enough resources to the secondary modern and primary schools to prevent them falling even further behind the new comprehensive as well as the independent, direct grant and grammar schools ? What can be done to dramatically increase the numbers of young working class people benefiting from further education ?

There are many other spheres in which there are sharp contrasts in facilities and opportunities. How is it possible to upgrade ancient hospitals, particularly for the chronic sick and mentally ill, when the general and teaching hospitals are insisting on new space and better equipment ? How can that proportion of slum and sub-standard housing which cannot be replaced in the next 20 years be renovated or modernised ? And how can the division of resources between different regions be prevented from remaining as unequal as it is or from becoming more unequal, despite the actions of recent governments ? In many different spheres therefore there is a problem not only of how to allocate additional resources but how to reallocate existing resources.

Some economists have suggested that emigration of labour from certain areas may have secondary depressing effects which perpetuate or even widen disparities between regions in unemployment rates (for example, G. C. Archibald "Regional Multiplier Effects in the United Kingdom," *Oxford Economic Papers*, Spring, 1967). Sociologists too have begun to call attention to these disparities. Over a period of eight years up to 1961 the number of long-term unemployed was on average ten times greater in the Northern Region than in the Eastern and Southern Regions. There was also a higher rate of sickness and incapacity, markedly lower average earnings and markedly fewer children staying on at school beyond the age of 15. (R. A. Sinfield, *Unemployed in Shields,* to be published)

In some respects, as I have suggested above, the problem of poverty in Britain has been growing. We can begin with low earnings. Unfortunately it is difficult to say much about the trends in the *distribution* of earnings over the past 20 years. But *average* earnings in low-paid industries are rising less quickly than in other industries. In 1960 the Ministry of Labour listed average earnings in 128 industries. There were 24 with average earnings of less than £12 10s. In 17 of these earnings rose during the next 6 years (April 1960 to April 1966) by less than the average of 44 per cent. Earnings in agriculture, which are also relatively low and which were excluded from this analysis, also rose less than average. (Ministry of Labour, *Statistics on Incomes, Prices, Employment and Production,* no 18, September 1966, pp 26-27)

Secondly, the value of family allowances has fallen. For a family with four children, for example, they have fallen from 12 per cent of average earnings in 1956 to 6 per cent of average earnings in 1966.

Thirdly, social security beneficiaries have continued to be subject to principles of "minimum" treatment, despite the development in this country of fringe benefits and fiscal welfare, despite more public awareness of the deprivations of environment and opportunity and despite the more rapid growth of social security in other countries. Levels of benefit have remained low. Between 1950 and 1960, as Mr. Tony Lynes has shown, average disposable income per head rose faster than national assistance rates. (*National Assistance and National Prosperity,* Occasional Papers on Social Administration, no 5, Codicote, 1962). Increases in benefits in 1961, 1962 and 1963 slightly redressed the balance, but not enough to do more than mildly improve the relative level of living of beneficiaries. And the position has worsened again since the latest increase which took place in March 1965.

Fourthly, the relative increase in dependence within the social structure, particularly children and the elderly, has swelled the numbers with low incomes. The numbers of children in large families and of persons of advanced age have increased disproportionately. Between 1953 and 1965 the number of children in families drawing family allowances in Britain grew by 25 per cent. But the number of fourth children attracting allowances in families grew by 50 per cent, fifth children by 63 per cent and sixth or later children by 84 per cent. (*Reports of the Ministry of Pensions and National Insurance for the years* 1953 *and* 1965, Cmd 9159 and Cmnd 3046, HMSO, 1954 and 1966) Also between 1953 and 1965 the number of retirement pensions in payment increased by 54 per cent. This rate of increase was faster than the increase in numbers of persons of pensionable age, which itself was much faster than the increase in the population of all ages. Two further points are worth noting. First, there has been a disproportionate increase in the numbers of persons aged 80 and over among the elderly; between 1951 and 1961 for example, their numbers increased by 40 per cent. Second, the Registrar General's estimates of population suggest that during the next 10 years the numbers of children under 15 and persons of pensionable age will increase by 15 or 16 per cent, but the population aged 15 to 59 will increase by only 2 per cent.

Sociologists have begun to write of an " underclass " in industrial societies and have also begun to appreciate that periodic increases in immigration can postpone the need to make structural adjustments in the economy and in the status hierarchy. Racial prejudices may displace but also in some ways reinforce existing social prejudices. White natives who occupy the same areas and kind of jobs as coloured immigrants can easily be regarded as inferiors too and gradually they experience a fall, relative to others, in living standards. There is therefore the possibility of poverty growing in two forms—that of a dependent " underclass " of persons who are found in all regions of the country, and that of immigrant and native-born families living in communities in areas of bad housing where the unemployment rate is high.

poor nutrition

Many illustrations of the consequences of these trends might be given. In the analysis of the data from the National Food Survey households are divided according to composition and social class into a number of groups. The proportion of children living in groups of households which consume a diet which *on average* fails in at least two particulars to reach the minimum levels recommended by the British Medical Association increased between 1960 and 1964 from 36 per cent to 43 per cent. Those in households failing to reach the minimum levels in three or four respects (protein, calcium, energy value and riboflavin) increased slightly from 16 per cent to 19 per cent.

This trend has not been consistent throughout the last 10 years. In 1956, for example, the number of children in families which on average failed to reach the minimum levels in two or more respects was 36 per cent, but in 3 or 4 respects 29 per cent. There has been a slow upward drift in the nutritive content of the average diet of all groups of families but (a) the poorest and largest groups of families have not gained on the richest and smallest families, (b) the poorest and some of the middle-income large families and those with adolescents and children have still to attain the BMA levels, and (c) relatively *more* of the children in the annual survey are now to be found in larger households. (Ministry of Agriculture, Fisheries and Food, *Domestic food consumption and expenditure,* 1964 *and* 1960, Annual reports of the National Food Survey, HMSO, 1966 and 1962).

The household groups with poor nutrition consist of man and wife and three or four children and families with adolescents and children and they include two groups in the highest income class, and not only groups with low incomes. I wish it were possible to express these findings more directly and more cogently. It is a public scandal that the National Food Survey Committee has as yet made no effort to establish the numbers and kinds of families markedly *below* the average. A national food survey has been carried out annually at considerable public expense for many years. Its most important conclusion has been buried in statistical minutiae. Although the conclusion was disinterred recently by curious social scientists and brought into public view (for example, R. Lambert, *Nutrition in Britain* 1950-60, Occasional Papers on Social Administration, no 6, Codicote, 1964) the Committee has not felt it proper either to present the findings in the most revealing form or to undertake urgent inquiries to develop our knowledge about these large sections of the population who are living at inferior nutritional levels. Perhaps the Ministers of Social Security, Labour and Agriculture can combine to put pressure on the Committee to answer the simple question which has been waiting to be answered for at least a decade—how many families (and how many children and adults in those families) have diets which are 10 per cent or 20 per cent or more below the minimum levels recommended by the British Medical Association?

INTENTIONS AND PERFORMANCE

By the late 1950's the Labour Party had begun to develop a coherent strategy for dealing with poverty. Of the statements published in the few years before October 1964, the most radical was probably *Signposts for the Sixties.* Measures were required to achieve two major objectives—the elimination in so many departments of national life of the disjunction between private affluence and public squalor and the dispersal of new forms of privilege or power that were concentrating among a small ruling elite. What were the remedies? They were, briefly, to transfer the freehold of building land to public ownership, repeal the Rent Act, repair and modernise private rented houses and build more houses, introduce redundancy payments, completely re-cast national insurance by introducing " a system of all-in wage-related social security," reduce the size of school classes, reorganise secondary schools along comprehensive lines " broaden the present narrow apex of higher education," establish a trust to integrate private with state schools, introduce a capital gains tax and re-grade family allowances steeply according to age. " We should reorganise family allowances, graduating them according to the age of the child, with a particularly steep rise for those remaining at school after the statutory school-leaving age." (*Signposts for the Sixties*, 1961)

Later statements added or reaffirmed plans for regions within a national economic plan, the introduction of an Incomes Guarantee and a rates rebate scheme, the abolition of prescription charges and the expansion of community care services. Writing at the time of the 1959 election, the present Prime Minister acknowledged the fact that " many " of the British people faced " real, bitter poverty." He went on " the co-existence of conspicuous wealth and avoidable poverty is a distortion of the moral laws of civilised society." He admitted that Labour's was a " piecemeal " programme but that it was " on a broad front " and corresponded with the complexities of human needs. Piecemeal though it was it represented " the unifying and transforming influence of a Socialist approach." (H. Wilson, " The war on poverty," *New Statesman*, 3 October 1959).

Whether these proposals were indeed sufficiently far-reaching and sufficiently integrated to meet the problem can of course be disputed. They were at least constructive and implied a shift of resources from rich to poor and from private to public sectors. But it must be emphasised that in the event the Labour Government has so far failed to implement some of the most important of these measures and has implemented others in a much milder form than originally intended. Let me be specific. In some instances the situation is clear. Measures like improved family allowances just have not been introduced. Measures like the Land Commission Bill, the Rent Act, the Capital Gains tax, the Corporation tax and the Social Security Act seem to be small in their effects. The Land Commission Bill turns a plan for the automatic acquisition of land for development (which meant stabilising rather than reducing the price of land) into one primarily involving a betterment levy. Power to acquire land in certain circumstances is vested in the commission but in the absence of evidence that it can be used extensively we must assume it will be used sparingly. The Commission is to be voted £45 million for acquiring and managing land and this would be extended to £75 million with Parliamentary approval. These are very small amounts by comparison with land values or capital investment programmes. It is of course too early to pronounce on the total effects of the bill, for much will depend on the policy which is in practice followed by the Commission, but the prospects of it becoming a major instrument in controlling development in the public interest are not dazzling. The Rent Act has damped down the increase in number of extortionate rents but by leaving initiative with tenants and creating a system of rent assessment which in some ways is biassed against tenants it has so far had a surprisingly small result. Moreover, many of those entitled to benefit under the new rates rebate scheme are not applying. The capital gains tax replaces the short-term levy introduced by Selwyn Lloyd. The maximum rate of 30 per cent (20 per cent for amounts up to £5,000) is low and is lower than the effective rate of income tax and surtax that is applicable to high incomes. This is not a wealth tax. It is an intermediate kind of tax which allows room for argument about some capital values at the time the Finance Act was implemented and therefore the amount of gain to which the rate of tax up to 30 per cent is applied.

social security

The incorporation of the income guarantee scheme within the Social Security Act is a particularly intriguing example of a paper lion which has turned into a lamb. For a long time the Labour Party had been searching for a way of abolishing the means test in national assistance, at least for the great majority of recipients, and simultaneously raising the standards of living of those who had been accustomed to drawing assistance. While in opposition in 1963 it stated, "As a result of the Government's policy, what was the exception had become the rule. . . . The means test, which it was the aim of the 1946 Act to abolish, has been built into the Government's system of social security, as one of its main instruments for distributing relief" (the Labour Party, *New frontiers for social security*, p9, 1963) In 1963 the Party therefore not only reaffirmed its previous support for a national superannuation scheme but firmly committed itself to extending the change " from flat-rate pensions to half-pay on retirement " to all forms of state benefits and, to ensure " fair play " for existing pensioners, an income guarantee was to be introduced. The guarantee involved giving a supplement to pensioners and widows to raise their incomes to a certain level " well in excess " of the present level of retirement pension. It would be paid automatically—through simplified tax returns.

The Social Security Act of 1966 attempts to preserve this proposal, but it is a pale shadow of its former self. Nominally the National Assistance Board has been abolished by the merger with the Ministry of Pensions. In its place is the Supplementary Benefits Commission. Efforts are being made to improve the image and encourage more people to apply for supplementary help. In some ways it is still too early to comment on administrative procedures. But the opportunity to make a clean break with restrictive and narrow-minded attitudes enshrined in the National Assistance Act of 1948 was lost. Some important steps in the direction of establishing the rights of non-contributory beneficiaries could have been taken. For example, it is a pity that the right of a person to know in writing how his supplementary benefit has been calculated or why his application for benefit has been refused was not written into the Act. The Minister gave assurances in committee that administratively " as soon as possible, at least those getting a supplementary pension (not *benefit*) will receive written explanation. Others, if there is a refusal, or if they are not clear, or if thy do not think that the amount they are receiving is sufficient will right from the beginning be able to ask for a written explanation, as they can do at the moment." (*Hansard,* 17 June 1966, col 1906) But the effect of a symbolic clause in the Act upon relations between officers of the new Commission and the public might have been considerable. Instead, much of the apparatus of the Act passed 18 years—almost a generation—previously has been preserved in a too bureaucratic form.

Secondly, the qualifying conditions for supplementary help were liberalised. The amounts of capital and income which can be " disregarded " in assessing needs was increased. A standard rate of 9s a week was added to the supplementary grants of old people and the sick. The idea was that this would be an automatic supplement for long-term beneficiaries. But for the great majority of existing recipients it made little or no difference to the amounts they received. Seventy-three per cent of supplementary pensioners at the end of 1965 were already receiving discretionary additions averaging 10s 1d per week. Fifty-seven per cent of the sick received amounts averaging 11s 8d. (*Report of the National Assistance Board for* 1965, *op cit,* p18). The 9s supplement does of course limit the amount of discretion that an officer can exercise at present to add to a particular rate of assistance. This is good but because the amount is so small it does not change the existing situation drastically. There will remain a large number of people whose incomes will in part depend on official discretion. And the opportunity the Government had of reviewing the rationale which should underlie the basic rates was not taken.

Thirdly, and most importantly, the income guarantee was not applied outside the customary spheres of operation of National Assistance. The Labour leaders wanted to fuse income tax and income security. But after they approached one of Britain's most implacable institutions, the Board of Inland Revenue, they retreated. Officials of this Board and of the National Assistance Board persuaded them to change their minds. Perhaps their momentum for reform had already been lost. The fact is that the Board of Inland Revenue felt it was outrageous for the Board actually to hand out money. Whoever heard of such an idea ? They were a taxation department, not a social service department. To bring together the functions of taxing income and making it more secure was most improper.

The verdict of history is likely to be that the Social Security Act of 1966 has achieved little more than extending national assistance, or supplementary benefit, to a larger number of the lower middle classes, while distinguishing rather more sharply between old and young. It has also served the purpose of saving face for the Labour Party—which is not perhaps the strongest reason for reform.

The Act also discriminates against the unemployed. One discriminatory practice against those with large families, the wage-stop, is preserved. Another, against the long-term unemployed, is introduced. Unlike the retired, who receive it at once, and unlike the sick, who receive it after two years, none of the unemployed receive the long-term benefit of 9s a week.

postponed superannuation

What has happened to the complementary and even more important plan—the wage-related scheme of social security, incorporating national superannuation ? I believe it can be argued that with a little more determination on the part of the Government we might have had this on the statute book by the end of 1965. In November 1964, soon after the election, the Government took a major decision. it announced big increases in existing benefits, raising the retirement pension of a single person by 12s 6d to £4 a week and of a married couple by 21s to £6 10s. This was, it is true, a substantial improvement on existing rates but was carried out within the structural inadequacies of the existing scheme and was quickly overtaken by earnings. The increase in early 1965 represented the largest *absolute* increase in insurance benefits, though some increases in earlier years were *relatively* larger. The benefits represented increases of 18.5 per cent for a single person and 19 per cent for a married couple but between May 1963 (when benefits were last increased) and August 1966 average industrial earnings rose by 20 per cent. Between May 1963 and August 1966 retail prices increased by 13 per cent. (*Ministry of Labour Gazette*, October 1966) Moreover, the employees' flat-rate contributions which, according to the Labour Party only a year earlier had " already reached a level where they constitute a savage poll tax on the lowest paid worker" (Labour Party, *New frontiers for social security*, p11) were increased by 17 per cent from 11s 8d to 13s 8d a week. One view was that the needs of the poor were urgent and that a comprehensive review would take time. But the work of Lord Beveridge's Committee in the war from the start to the publication of the actual report was accomplished in eleven months and the Labour Government already had a head start afforded by the deliberations and publications of its Study Group on Security and Old Age, which had been sitting since the mid-fifties. Another view is that it had difficulty in getting on with a socialist programme with such a tiny Parliamentary majority and in such a grave economic crisis. But the social productivity, if we may call it such, of the Labour Government has been if anything smaller since March 1966 than before that date, and the National Plan, as Brian Abel-Smith has pointed out, actually adopted the assumption that a major new scheme would not be introduced before 1969.

In fact, what was planned to be a consistent and concerted attack on poverty has turned into haphazard skirmishes on a wide front. The Government has given little impression from its actions that it has adopted an overall strategy. By increasing benefits along conventional lines early in 1965 it took the edge off demands for reform. By then introducing a redundancy payments Act and later earnings-related benefit in unemployment and sickness for the first six months it allowed itself to be diverted from giving priority to poverty to giving priority to redeployment. The earnings-related scheme for the unemployed and sick does little for those with low earnings. Men and women with less than £9 a week do not qualify. A man with £12 a week gets a supplement of £1 in addition to his flat-rate benefit of £4 but if he has a wife and four children only 8 shillings because the Act has introduced a maximum total benefit of 85 per cent of earnings and, with a flat-rate of £9 16s, he would otherwise exceed this maximum. If he is unlucky enough to have been unemployed or sick for a total of twelve weeks in the preceding tax year, by no means a rare eventuality, he will receive no supplement at all. Adrian Sinfield also points out that " the implication of calculating gross *weekly* earnings from a gross *annual* income for the assessment of the supplement seems to have been overlooked. Although the use of a gross annual income has administrative advantages, it also lowers the value of the supplement for men with previous recent experience of unemployment, sickness or any other absence from work." (*Unemployed in Shields,* to be published).

The scheme does nothing for the man with long-term benefit. The supplement is paid after two weeks unemployment but ceases after a further six months. Those who have become accustomed to receiving fairly substantial earnings-related supplements will then experience a sharp reduction in level of living. If they are sick and draw means-tested supplementation they have to wait another 18 months before they qualify for a standard supplement of 9s a week. This is not planning. It is helter-skelter chaos. There are a number of connected problems. The Government has failed to wind up the Conservative Government's graduated pension scheme, after proclaiming, rightly, that it was a disgraceful " swindle." The benefits are very small indeed in relation to contributions. The Government's " profit " on the scheme is growing. In 1962-3 the excess of income over expenditure was £182 million, in 1964-5 it was £277 million. (Parliamentary written answer by Mr. Norman Pentland, *Hansard,* 6 July 1965). The Government has also failed to introduce transferability of pension rights, which means incidentally that it has not removed an important obstacle to redeployment.

Instead of a co-ordinated and consistent scheme of social security we run the risk of building up a fragmented, piecemeal set of measures which bristle with anomalies and between which many groups in the population fall. It should perhaps be recalled that the original aim of the Labour Party's national super-annuation plan, and hence of the comprehensive wage-related social security plan, was to bring about a dramatic immediate increase (50 per cent for single retire-ment pensioners) in national insurance benefits by rationalising the principles and practises of existing employers, private and public schemes within a single wage-related scheme which the mass of the population might find personally attractive as well as socially just. (The Labour Party, *National Superannuation*, 1957). The scheme would simultaneously reduce by over a million the number having to depend in any form on means-tested assistance. The introduction of a single co-ordinated scheme would also allow more flexibility than a succession of piece-meal measures to eliminate anomalies. Perhaps the most indefensible of these is the payment of different rates of benefit to those disabled in war, industry and civil life.

sub-standard housing

Let me refer briefly to one other plan. Has much been done to carry out the modernisation and repair of sub-standard housing? According to the Denington sub-committee on standards of housing fitness, which reported in November 1966, "there are many, many houses which are below any standard that can be con-sidered satisfactory in the second half of the twentieth century. About three-quarters of a million are below the present minimum fitness standard. Something like 3 million lack one or more of the basic amenities of water closet, cold water tap, hot water supply and bath. While some of them will be demolished in the next few years, others must serve for a longer period, however fast new homes are built. These must have some degree of improvement, according to the length of time they will remain in use. Sound houses must be maintained in good repair and improved where practicable. Successive governments have tried to secure the voluntary modernisation of these houses but the response has been inadequate and disappointing. Present measures of compulsion, which apply in limited cir-cumstances to tenanted property, have proved ineffective, perhaps because of the cumbersome and time consuming procedure. *In our view there is a need both for effective compulsion to improve and maintain the better old houses and for more pressure for early clearance of the worst.*" (Ministry of Housing, Central Housing Avisory Committee, *Our Older Homes: A Call for Action*, Report of the sub-committee on standards of housing fitness, p5, HMSO, 1966).

Although about 120,000 improvement grants a year in England and Wales are made, only about a third are made to private landlords. The principal beneficiaries are middle-class owner-occupiers.

While some Government actions have not lived up to pre-election plans others may actually have reinforced social inequalities and poverty. For example, soon after awarding Members of Parliament, Ministers and judges huge proportionate pay increases and university teachers, general practitioners and senior civil servants increases ranging from 10 to 25 per cent the Government expected the trade unions to happily accept a wage-policy holding down increases to 3 to 4 per cent. The restoration of traditional differentials of pay can be invoked to justify most of these increases. But in terms of long-term socialist strategy as well as the immediate need to secure support for an incomes policy they were inept.

Again, by imposing harsh controls on the entry of immigrants and by simultaneously refraining from introducing any really positive measures for racial integration, the moral authority of the Labour Party, so carefully established by Hugh Gaitskell in the famous Parliamentary debates of 1961 and 1962, was lost in one reckless step. The position of the coloured minority is still very different in Britain from what it is in the United States but social scientists are beginning to wonder whether we will follow the pattern established there of increasing inequality in living standards and employment status between white and coloured sections of the population. Research has shown that in the years since the war the economic gains of the non-white population in the United States have been less than proportional to those of whites, and that the relative position of a significant majority of non-whites has worsened. (O. Ornati, *op cit*, p59). If so, then Britain will have, if it has not already, a group of new poor. By adopting a non-existent or at most a weak policy on the integration of coloured immigrants the Government has surrendered more than it probably realises. Acquiescence in racial inequality tends to have a corrupting influence on general attitudes towards social inequalities.

FUTURE POLICIES

This analysis clearly implies certain priorities in policy. First of all, measures to raise low standards of living are required. The most urgent action is required to greatly increase family allowances (by at least threefold) and extend them to first children in the family. In a recent survey of 62 countries with some form of family allowances system, only 12 were found not to make a payment to the first or only child in the family. (United States Department of Health, Education and Welfare, *Social security throughout the world*, 1964, Washington 1966). General pensions and allowances including constant attendance allowances must be introduced for the long-term sick and those disabled in civil life as well as in

64

industry and war. The Disablement Income Group has been bringing the needs to the attention of the public. (The anomalies of social security benefits have been discussed recently by Mrs. Phyllis Willmott in a book written otherwise by disabled individuals P. Hunt (ed), *Stigma: The Experience of Disability*, Chapman, 1966). Some form of regular State maintenance allowances for all fatherless families must also be introduced and the wage-stop in the supplementary benefit and earnings-related unemployment and sickness schemes abolished.

The more comprehensive plan for wage-related social security must be brought forward. A major repairs and modernisation programme is badly needed, particularly for housing (Ministry of Housing, Central Advisory Committee, *Our Older Homes, op cit*) as I have argued, but also for schools and hospitals, quite apart from a scheme for new building which involves an expenditure closer to the proportions of gross national product being spent by some other countries. (See, for example, Political and Economic Planning, Broadsheet no 490, *Housing in Britain, France and Western Germany*, 1965, United Nations, *Statistical indicators of housing levels of living* 1959). A variety of measures to strengthen the threadbare sections of our social services are also required. Examples of these are under-doctored areas and under-developed community-care services, under-staffed schools, particularly secondary modern schools where there is a high turnover of staff, and under-staffed hospitals, particularly those for long-stay patients.

universalism

Second, because the new minimum levels can be defined only in relation to the resources, customs and institutions of the community, certain complementary measures must simultaneously be adopted to reallocate those resources and modify those customs and institutions. These will inevitably form part of general domestic policy. It means challenging the kind of view put forward by the Minister of Social Security at the 1966 Labour Party Conference when she said that further improvements in social security depended on economic productivity. Other social service Ministers have made similar statements. The argument was put forward in the Labour Party Election Manifesto of 1964. In fact, of course, there is considerable scope for redistribution, of both an aggregate nature from one public service to another as well as of a vertical nature between well-off and poor, even at a time of economic crisis. Fundamentally redistribution must also be reinforced by change in political and administrative institutions. "A new Government unhappily does not mean a new Civil Service elite. . . . The Civil Service is too narrowly based on Oxbridge. It lacks expertise. The specialists it has are not put in the right places; its personnel lacks experience in the industrial, financial and social service fields in which is has to operate; there are high institutional barriers to outside recruitment; it neglects to train." (P. Shore, *Entitled to Know*, p154, MacGibbon and Kee, 1966).

The tax system must be more progressive. Its total effect is in fact regressive at the lowest incomes and then proportional even up to quite high incomes at present. In 1964 a family of man and wife and two children with an original income in the lower middle range of £676 to £815 paid about 28 per cent of that income in taxes (national insurance contributions 9 per cent, income tax 1 per cent and indirect taxes 18 per cent) while a similar family with an income of £1448 to £1751 paid 27 per cent (national insurance 5 per cent, income tax 7 per cent and indirect taxes 15 per cent). For a family of man and wife and one child the figures are 32 and 32 respectively and for a man and wife and three children 25 and 24 respectively. For families of similar composition *direct* taxes are mildly progressive from 100 per cent below to 100 per cent above the mean income, *indirect* taxes are mildly regressive and national insurance contributions sharply regressive. (These figures are based on tables D, 1d and 2b in " The incidence of taxes and social service benefits in 1963 and 1964," *Economic Trends*, no 154, August 1966. In calculating the percentage of original income taken in indirect taxes, I have taken the total of indirect taxes on all income and have divided it proportionately between the income remaining after taxes and insurance contributions have been paid and income represented by social service cash benefits, that is family allowances and national insurance benefits).

Real income re-distribution does not seem to have markedly changed since before the war. " There appears to have been little increase in the amount of vertical redistribution between 1937 and 1959, but the extent of the increase, if any, depends on how much the estimates of the amount of redistribution in 1937 would have been reduced if they had been made on the same basis as our estimates. for 1959." (J. L. Nicholson, *Redistribution of income in the United Kingdom in 1959, 1957 and 1953*, Bowes and Bowes, 1965).

If tax allowances for children are reduced, and direct family allowances increased, and if wage-related contributions replace flat-rate contributions in social security some but not all of the inequalities will be reduced as they affect relatively low income groups. Other measures to strengthen the progressiveness of the tax system become necessary. It is possible, in the history of tax policy, that when certain groups in the population are taxed more heavily they respond by asking for larger pay differentials and by resorting more frequently to legal and illegal methods of avoiding tax, by pressing for larger fringe benefits and by converting income into capital. Much of this therefore implies that egalitarian objectives must be pursued more vigorously through fiscal policy but also through measures designed to elicit information particularly from companies, corporations and trade unions and impose limits on their powers to exploit privilege. The new Companies Act is a mild step in this direction.

I am arguing, in effect, that some form of incomes policy is necessary less for economic than for social reasons. Minimum wage legislation might be helpful in raising the standards of those with the lowest wages, but only if it is wide in scope and if the levels are not merely linked automatically with average earnings but deliberately designed to *rise,* relative to the average, over a number of years. Economists have come to mixed conclusions about minimum wage legislation.

For example, a review of the 1956 American legislation suggested that *temporary* improvements were secured in low-wage industries at the cost of some displacement of labour and a reversion before long to former differentials (N. M. Douty, " Some effects of the $1 minimum wage in the United States," *Economica,* May 1960). One assumption upon which a new national plan should be based is that minimum wages and minimum social security benefits will in future rise faster than average earnings. Poverty must be tackled through a wages or incomes policy as much as through a better fiscal or social security policy.

This amounts therefore to an argument for a deliberate policy of securing a levelling up of wage and income levels through a concerted incomes, fiscal and social security policy. It means bringing certain Government departments together which are not accustomed to working with each other. It also means professionalising the Civil Service and improving the information at our disposal. Earlier I complained about the analyses offered by the National Food Survey Committee. There is little doubt that far better analyses of income distribution could be provided through the Board of Inland Revenue and the Ministry of Labour than are at present published. We are just beginning to produce the kind of data which are needed by a modern society if it is to have humanitarian and socialist objectives. This needs emphasising for it is no academic foible. If the Ministry of Pensions had had a substantial Statistical and Research Department in the past the reluctance of hundreds of thousands of beneficiaries to apply for assistance, or the poverty of children in large families and of the disabled, might have been revealed a lot earlier. Perhaps the newly-appointed Director of the Central Statistical Office can, with suitable support from Ministers, breathe sweetness and light into the innermost recesses of the Government's information services.

limitation of privileges

Finally, however, this strategy of achieving equality through integration cannot be effective unless it is recognised that adjustments have to be expected of social elites. If poverty is relative then standards are partly determined by the incomes, wealth, living conditions and expectations of the rich. The relief of poverty is secured by lower managerial and professional incomes, relative to the average, as much as by higher minimum wages and benefits. It is not that the rich can pay sufficient new taxes to finance, say, a major increase in the retirement pension. It is doubtful whether they could finance a five shilling increase. Their resources and incomes provide the starting point from which the rest of the social hierarchy unfolds, and this is crucial. No doubt the difficulties of embarking upon such a strategy are immense. History might lead us to suppose that although there are periods of greater social equality the traditional lines of division between classes and income groups reappear in the long run. Guy Routh made a detailed study of occupational and pay structure in Britain between 1906 and 1960 and concluded that over a period of 50 years " the most impressive finding was the rigidity of the inter-class and inter-occupational relationships." "According to our calculations, the average for semi-skilled men was 86 per cent of the all-class average in 1913 and 85 per cent in 1960; (G. Routh, *Occupation and Pay in Great Britain,* px, Cambridge, University Press, 1965). Certain comparative figures drawn from the same source are equally interesting. In 1913/14 the unskilled worker received approximately 19 per cent of the average earnings of " higher " professional workers (16 per cent of general practitioners' average earnings) and in 1960 26 per cent (21 per cent). In 1913/14 he earned 31 per cent of the average earnings of managers but in 1960 29 per cent. (G. Routh, *ibid,* calculated from tables 30 and 47). Barbara Wootton has brilliantly described the apparently irrational but fundamentally social determination of differentials of pay. (Barbara Wootton, *The Social foundations of wage policy,* Allen and Unwin, London, second edition, 1967).

The problem, moreover, is no longer narrowly national. The " brain drain " and the emulation by elites in developing countries of western standards of living reminds us that the inequalities of pay structures have outside determinants as well. But difficult as it is the problem must be faced. Government Ministers should have relatively lower salaries than they do today. So should Permanent Secretaries, university professors, hospital consultants and company directors. If maximum wage-legislation is felt to be remote from political practicalities I believe it will in time come to be taken seriously. In struggling to establish the principle of making public the remuneration of company directors and managers, Peter Shore, among others, has recognised that incomes policy must start at the top. " The top salary structure (of industry) . . . is today shrouded in secrecy and has never been subject to any serious or rational consideration." (P. Shore, *Hansard,* 21 February 1966). The moral point which I want to impress is that if it is the highly skilled, managerial and professional classes who gain from present differentials it is the aged, the low-wage earners, the children in large families, the sick and the disabled who lose.

In advanced industrial societies inequalities are maintained by the educational system, by the institutions of property and inheritance, by the professions and the trade unions, and by popular ideas or beliefs about status, responsibility and rights. The process of structural change can introduce new inequalities as well as reduce existing ones. Every salary increase that is larger than the average wage-increase, even when accepted by national sentiment to retain the professional manpower, say, of doctors and scientists, widens inequalities and may indirectly increase the extent of poverty. One is linked to the other. The privileges at the exclusive public school are gained at the cost of worse conditions in a secondary modern school in one of our big cities. One is in equilibrium with the other. So perhaps the critical criterion of socialist strategy, which the Government has yet to meet, is a relative diminution of the citadels of privilege. When honours are no longer conferred, and managers earn only two or three times as much as dustmen, and, cruellest of all, public schools really are integrated rather than given a new lease of life by Flemingism, the millenium may begin to dawn.

I have been extremely critical of the Government's record in the first two years of office. It would be unfair to neglect the list of reforms which have been adopted —the abolition of prescription charges, the tax on betting, the restriction on business expenses, protection from eviction and others in addition to some which I have discussed. Good deeds have been done. But they are no more than hot compresses on an ailing body politic. I have tried to call attention to the need for a more single-minded and large-scale strategy to achieve greater social equality and have tried to make a number of constructive suggestions. I have argued that greater equality is not dependent on economic growth. Indeed it would be possible to go further and argue that greater equality is a pre-condition for rapid economic growth. National morale can be raised and the right sense of national purpose created. Improving social security could be one means of persuading people to accept severe restraint on wage and salary increases. Another could be further control of upper-income fringe benefits and tax avoidance practices. These suggest what would be a practical immediate policy as well as one concordant with ultimate socialist objectives. The Labour Government is compromising too readily with entrenched interests, is avoiding the need to confront racial and social prejudice with moral authority, is failing to introduce institutional change and is forgetting that in this growingly more complicated world it must, like Alice, run even faster to stay in the same place and to preserve, still less extend, existing human rights.

Partly our problem is one with which it is irresponsible to pretend that Government Ministers must wrestle alone. Tawney reminded us, " Nothing could be more remote from Socialist ideals than the competitive scramble of a society which pays lip service to equality, but too often means by it merely equal opportunities of becoming unequal." He warned against "the corrupting influence of a false standard of values, which perverts, not only in education, but wide tracts of thought and life. It is this demon—the idolatry of money and success—with whom, not in one sphere alone but in all, including our own hearts and minds, Socialists have to grapple." (R. H. Tawney, *The Radical Tradition,* pp 178-180, Allen and Unwin, 1964).

socialism and planning

R. H. S. Crossman

I wish to reply to the arguments of Brian Abel-Smith in his essay *Labour's social plans* and Peter Townsend in *Poverty, Socialism and Labour in power*, and in so doing to render an interim account of what the Government has, and has not, achieved, particularly in dealing with the problems of poverty. In doing so I cannot forget that my education in this particular problem was largely carried out by Richard Titmuss, Brian Abel-Smith and Peter Townsend. In 1956 I was made chairman of the working party on social security at Transport House and at once made one of the most useful decisions of my life by inviting the three to become members of it. As a result we worked together very closely for quite a time—and in the course of those years we not only did the detailed research work on which *National superannuation* and *New frontiers of social security* were based : we also evolved what was then a new critical attitude towards the whole Beveridge philosophy. The more we reflected on the social security legislation which resulted from the Beveridge plan, the more we realised how backward looking it was. Everything was conceived in terms of the concentrated areas of mass unemployment and the grey climate of working class poverty which hung over the 1930s. Flat-rate contributions and flat-rate benefits derived from the notion of flat-rate equality—the pessimistic determination to ensure that since poverty was endemic, poverty must at least be fairly shared.

From this critique of Lord Beveridge we moved quite naturally to a critique of another personality whose philosophy has come to dominate his epoch, J. K. Galbraith. In many ways we took *The affluent society* as the basis of our discussions; but we realized that he had made one profoundly serious mistake—to suggest that, as the modern community grows steadily wealthier under technological advances, poverty ceases to be a significant problem. Since then, of course, in America there have been plenty of witnesses to indicate the width and the depth of poverty even in that most affluent society; indeed the President largely won the last election by promulgating his plan for abolishing that poverty. But what we were trying to do was not related to the United States. We were working out a policy for the British Opposition, preparing for a change of government here which then seemed pretty remote, and trying to ensure that if ever that change came a Labour Government would have the policies at hand to deal with this problem. It is, therefore, right and proper that we should discuss in these autumn lectures how the policies we developed in that working party have stood the test of time; how far they have been implemented by the Labour Government, and, in particular, whether it has shown itself equipped to cope with the problems of poverty in affluence.

the indictment

In a sense the reader is the judge and jury here. I represent the defendant while the three professors are the prosecutors presenting their indictment. For there is no doubt about it, their essays, taken together, do form an indictment of Government policy. Though we have only been in office two years and have got four more years to run, they have come to the conclusion that as a Government we have already failed to carry out the policies with which they are specially concerned. Despite the shortness of the time they have written us off and ask you to deliver your verdict upon us.

Let me remind you of the terms of their indictment. Peter Townsend says we have abandoned our long-term strategy, if we ever had one, and he adds that we have also failed in the short term. This is what he says about our short-term programme. "Whether these proposals were indeed sufficiently far-reaching and sufficiently integrated to meet the problem can of course be disputed. They were at least constructive and implied a shift of resources from rich to poor and from private to public sectors. But it must be emphasised that in the event the Labour Government has so far failed to implement some of the most important of these measures and has implemented others in a much milder form than originally intended. Let me be specific. In some instances the situation is clear. Measures like improved family allowances just have not been introduced. Measures like the Land Commission Bill, the Rent Act, the Capital Gains tax, the Corporation tax and the Social Security Act seem to be small in their effects." (p57)

Just a moment's pause here for reflection. I shall have something to say about the Rent Act in a moment. Meanwhile it is not my impression that our opponents— the people whose economic interests are vitally effected—regard these measures as "small in their effects." It seems to me surprising that our friends should feel so sure of themselves in dismissing them already as trivial and ineffective although it will be a couple of years at least before it will be possible to make any detailed assessment of how the first batch of our legislation, condemned by our opponents as a reckless inroad into private capitalism, is actually working.

Although Brian Abel-Smith was just as vehement I find his essay rather more constructive. I find myself in a good deal of sympathy, for example, with the section "Why limit social spending?" in which he points to the dangers of keeping public expenditure rigidly down to $4\frac{1}{4}$ per cent a year at constant prices "while turning a blind eye to tax allowances and private occupational social security, health and welfare benefits." (p19) He gives a tough warning to Ministers against the danger of letting themselves be straight-jacketed by a system of accounting which strictly rations the increase of state pensions while subjecting occupational benefits to no restraint; or (to take another example) which treats the provision by local authorities of rented houses as public expenditure which ought to be severely rationed, whereas the building of houses for sale is treated as the kind of private sector growth which ought to be encouraged. Programming of this style strangles progress. If we are to plan our social programme sensibly we must first decide how much of our national resources we devote to each part of the programme. A second, and much more difficult stage, comes when, within each part, we try to strike the proper balance between, for example, houses to rent and houses to sell, or between state pensions and private occupational schemes.

I now turn to his central theme which is equally stimulating. Far too few people bothered to read the National Plan before they condemned it. Brian Abel-Smith read it, digested it, discovered things in it that I did not know were there and drew what, for socialists, must at first sight have been disturbing conclusions. Taking the actual figures for 1958-64 and comparing them with the planned figures for 1965-70 he showed that the gap between private spending and social spending was planned to narrow more slowly under the Labour Government than it actually narrowed under the Tories. *The National Plan,* he commented "makes extraordinarily little provision for narrowing the gap between private affluence and public squalor." (p12) Turning his attention to individual services he expressed his disappointment at the targets set for housing, health, education and, in particular, social security where he extracted figures to show that the planned level of living of pensioners would fall behind that of wage-earners in such a way as to deny them the share of national prosperity to which the Labour Party Manifesto attached so much importance. Finally, analysing the global totals, he came to the conclusion that "the plan gave less than £1,000 million to public squalor and nearly £4,500 million to private affluence." (p16)

Professor Abel-Smith very fairly admits that, in drawing such conclusions, much depends on the period of Tory rule taken in comparison with the period of Labour planning. I would add that *The National Plan* was designed not as something fixed and settled and final but as a rolling programme to be reviewed every year. It may well be that the allocation of national resources to the social wage as distinct from personal incomes was too modest and, as the Plan was gradually accomplished, the Nation would have been prepared to see the increase in personal earnings slowed down in exchange for increased social benefits. The Plan, in fact, was not a categorical imperative laid down for five years ahead, it could always be reviewed and corrected. That a socialist government should, in this respect, err on the side of realism is surely a fault in the right direction.

I have quoted enough I think to give a fair impression of the tenor of the collective indictment. As I studied the lectures, what fascinated me (because in addition to being a politician I have also some training as an observer of politicians) was the width of the gap that had grown up between us in a matter of months. We have been less than two and a half years apart and yet we feel worlds apart. They criticise the Labour Government from a position in which they have little contact with the realities I experience every day. I look at the same problem from a point of view that so shocks them that they can hardly believe it is one their old friend has conscientiously adopted. How often in the old days we used to say that at all costs we must prevent things developing so that socialist intellectuals would be in one compartment and Labour politicians in another. That has happened already if I am to take what they have said here at its face value.

But is it the last word they have to say? I am still convinced it is not. Indeed what I am saying to them this evening is that before they finally come to their conclusions they should hear something of the practical problems the Government is facing in the field of social welfare, of the difficulties we have overcome and hope to overcome, and of the reasons why progress has varied on different parts of the front. When they were advising a party in opposition they had to be content to see the blueprints they first put forward radically modified to meet the objections of practical men of affairs. Perhaps something of the same sort has to occur when it is a question of collaboration between the academic and the Government.

intelligence deficiencies in Whitehall

I am going to start my reply, however, by stating my entire agreement with a large section of Peter Townsend's lecture. Indeed I reckon that in more than half of it he was concentrating his indignation on the scandalous absence of information upon which to base policy. Let me say this to him. I took the same view before I got into Government, and I take it far more strongly since I got there.

How I warmed when I read what he said, "It is a public scandal that the National Food Survey Committee has as yet made no effort to establish the numbers and kinds of families markedly *below* the average. A national food survey has been carried out annually at considerable public expense for many years. Its most important conclusion has been buried in statistical minutiae. Although the conclusion was disinterred recently by curious social scientists and brought into public view (for example, R. Lambert, *Nutrition in Britain*, 1950-60, Occasional Papers on Social Administration, no 6, Codicote, 1964) the Committee has not felt it proper either to present the findings in the most revealing form or to undertake urgent inquiries to develop our knowledge about these large sections of the population who are living at inferior nutritional levels." (p56) And then you can feel his exasperation with those of us who were once his allies in Opposition when he observes, "perhaps the Ministers for Social Security, Labour and Agriculture can combine to put pressure on the Committee to answer the simple questions that have been waiting to be answered for at least a decade, how many families have diets which are 10 per cent or 20 per cent or more below the minimum levels recommended by the British Medical Association?" (p56)

Of course he is right to be indignant. But is he right to be indignant with Ministers who have failed to put it right—in two years? I can only say that it is much more infuriating for us inside to be denied the information we require than it is for him outside. After all, for Ministers the absence of the essential facts may mean a tragically wrong decision whereas for him it usually connotes only the absence of a footnote.

Everybody knows the story Nye Bevan used to tell. Political power was his grail. He got himself elected to the Parish Council in order to find it but when he got into the Council Chamber it wasn't there. So he got himself elected first to the Urban District, then to the County and at last to Parliament and he couldn't find it anywhere in the Palace of Westminster. He fought his way into the Cabinet and then into the sanctum of the inner Cabinet—and always it had eluded him. Partly, perhaps, because I spent seven years as an Oxford don, my quest has been not so much for the secret place where power is concealed as for the Committee whose decisions are taken in the light of the available evidence. And all my life the vision has eluded me. Wherever I got myself elected, to the Fellows Meeting at New College, to my Faculty Meeting, to the Oxford City Council, to Parliament and, finally, to the Cabinet, the higher I climbed the more certain I was that on the next storey of the pyramid of power I would find a body of people making their decisions not on hunch and guesswork but on the basis of reliable information. Now I know that in Whitehall at least I was searching, not for a will o' the wisp, but for a pot of gold which is extremely difficult to find—except of course in wartime. In Eisenhower's Headquarters I caught sight of it for a year or two before peace broke out.

improvement areas

Of course the information available in Whitehall is still miserably inadequate! But it is a great deal better than it was two years ago. At least we have begun organising the flow. Let me give one example. In his lecture Peter Townsend bitterly complains because we have not yet launched a campaign to clean up the twilight areas of our cities and help landlords and tenants to improve the older houses which are not yet slums but which will, as things are going, become slums within a decade. He is quite right that the campaign has not yet been launched. First of all we had to fulfil our promises to annul the Tory Rent Act, to establish the Land Commission, to provide the local authorities with a housing subsidy which insulates them against rising interest rates, to help the owner-occupier with option mortgages. Because all these were in the programme the Cabinet naturally gave them a priority which improvement policy in the twilight areas did not enjoy. But one of my first actions as Minister of Housing was to call my Central Advisory Council together and get them to set up a working party which would review the situation and make urgent recommendations. The working party had a big job but its report was published in November 1966—the same month when Mr. Townsend was castigating the Government for dilatoriness. Apparently our crime was to await the information upon which sound policies can be based instead of adopting the usual British practice of deciding on hunch.

Of course a politician shouldn't always wait until all the evidence is available; if he does he may postpone his decision until history has taken it for him. But in this particular case it did seem reasonable to postpone action until we had collected the information. Partly we got it from the working party I mentioned; partly from the Deeplish study of Rochdale. To his eternal credit my predecessor had collected a highly specialised group of sociologists, engineers, architects and administrators to study one twilight area of a Lancashire town, house by house, family by family. For the first time both the actual fabric of the houses and the psychological fabric of family life inside the houses has been studied in detail in order to see exactly what happens in a twilight area, which is so far from being a slum that at the present rate of slum clearance it will still be there in 2010. We all have our hunches about the relative merits of a landlord and an owner-occupier when it comes to house maintenance and house improvement. In the Deeplish study we can compare those hunches with a set of facts. I won't pretend that either this study or *Our Older Homes* (Ministry of Housing Central Housing Advisory Committee, Report of the Sub-Committee on Standards of Housing Fitness, 1966) reveal anything very startling. What they do is to enable the Ministry to base its policies on relatively well-established fact.

housing statistics

Let me now turn to two other sectors of the Housing front, the first where the information is still miserably inadequate and the second where it is almost uniquely reliable. In his lecture Brian Abel-Smith was very scornful of the Government's target of 500,000 houses a year. He warns us all, that this is both inadequate in the face of the social need and humiliating when compared with the achievements of New Zealand, Switzerland, Sweden or even Italy and Greece which all devote a much higher percentage of the gross annual product to housing than we plan to achieve in 1970.

Of course it would be nice to wave a wand and be sure that in 12 months' time Britain was spending the $7\frac{1}{2}$ per cent now spent in Israel instead of the 3.9 per cent which the National Plan suggested as a five year goal. But in this country even the very modest switch we planned could only be achieved by drastic Government intervention designed to divert a part of a very small construction industry from its present variety of commercial enterprises into less profitable house building.

Before we could even contemplate the enlarged housing programme we had to take powers to control office building and apply them first in London and then in Birmingham. In addition we had to introduce building controls which enabled the Ministry of Public Building and Works to examine any project costing over £100,000 and decide whether to licence it or not.

But that was only the beginning of the job. During that last frantic election year of 1964 the aim of the Tory Government was to get the maximum number of houses built anywhere at any price. This was targeteering with a vengeance. When we took over we inherited a construction industry dangerously overheated, with soaring prices and soaring costs. We decided that targeteering must stop. With only limited resources available for housing we must build the right houses at the right price in the right places and this required precise accurate information about slums, overcrowding and the other factors in housing needs, very little of which was available. It is surely wrong for a socialist critic of the Government to deal solely in the global totals of houses built, without devoting a paragraph to the crucial balance that has to be struck between council houses to let and private houses for sale. And because he neglected this he failed to observe a second area where new research is desparately needed. Something has been done since 1964 but it is still true that neither the Minister of Housing nor the Chancellor of the Exchequer has a really accurate picture of the private sector of housing with the result that the attempt to predict the figures far ahead is like a sweepstake. Until now every Minister of Housing has been presented with an astonishing contrast between the public sector, which can be planned almost like a military operation, and the private sector, where production is at the mercy of market forces and interest rates. At last a serious study of the private sector is beginning. But until it gets a good deal further, Anthony Greenwood will be unable to base the strategy of his housing drive on the reliable statistical predictions available to the Minister of Housing in Sweden, for example.

Allen and Milner-Holland

Now let me turn to two areas of housing policy and two Acts of Parliament where the policy decisions *were* taken in the light of all the evidence available—the Rate Rebate Act and the Rent Act. In both these cases we were very lucky because excellently manned committees of enquiry had been set up by my predecessor. The Allen Committee had been able to base quite elaborate and detailed calculation on the results of an expensive social survey which revealed the incidence of rates on the various social classes and confirmed in particular the insupportable burden they imposed on families relying on small incomes, particularly old age pensioners. On the basis of this excellent report it was not difficult to work out remedies which we could be sure could be applied precisely where the shoe pinched hardest. Just as important, when it came to getting the bill through Parliament, the evidence provided by Professor Allen and his colleagues made it difficult for any reasonable person to oppose what we were doing. Professor Townsend's only comment on this measure is to complain that "many of those entitled to benefit under the new rate rebate scheme are not applying." (p58) Well the figures show that for the first half of the financial year about a million ratepayers received rebates averaging £7 12s 6d each. Bearing in mind that our rebates are designed, not for the poorest families who have their rates met in full through the social security system, but for the band just above the National Assistance level, this figure seems to me quite impressive.

His attitude to the Rent Act is equally unenthusiastic. "The Act" he remarks, "has damped down the increase in number of extortionate rents but, by leaving initiative with tenants and creating a system of rent assessment which in some ways is biased against tenants it has so far had a surprisingly small result." (p58) I must say I find this criticism curmudgeonly. Quite apart from providing machinery for revising rents the Act at once restored full security of tenure to nearly one million tenants of private landlords as well as providing for the first time in English history a minimum basic security against harassment and eviction for all occupants including those in lodgings and in tied cottages. I would very much hope that academic social scientists, particularly from the new departments in our new Universities, will do the investigation required to ascertain the effects on landlords as well as on tenants of this tenant's charter. I should like them also to give us a detailed study of the Rent Act's effect on the problem of homelessness, particularly in London. Before these researches have been published it would seem to me hazardous for anyone to claim knowledge that the Act "has so far had a surprisingly small result."

Professor Townsend singles out "the system of rent assessment" for special criticism. But since he believes as much as I do in basing policy on ascertained facts he should at least admit that this part of the Act was carefully based on the findings of the Milner-Holland Committee on London Housing. As soon as I read the first draft of that report I realised it was an object lesson of what intelligent and imaginative research can do for the practical politician. It provided us in the Ministry with all the information we required about the physical state of privately rented houses in London, about the levels of rent, about the conditions of the tenants and the behaviour of the landlords. It seemed to us that every one of the relevant questions had been asked by the Committee and that, thanks to the excellence of its expert staff and the thoroughness of the investigation, the picture they gave us was as complete and as reliable as human effort could make it. Moreover in all our main decisions we were able to use the members of the Committee as advisers and consultants, both in policy formulation—for example the definition of a fair rent—and in deciding on the quite novel division of responsibility between rent assessment committees and rent offices.

If there are faults in the Rent Act they are certainly not due either to lack of reliable information or to a failure to consult the best outside experts. Indeed it was on the basis of their social survey that we based all planning, on what seemed at the time the extremely hazardous assumption that even in London the vast majority of people living in privately rented houses were relatively contented and wouldn't demand a revision of their rent even if we established a tribunal and encouraged them to go to it. When our Civil Servants saw the figures in the survey (88 per cent relatively content, 12 per cent with a sense of injustice) some of them thought it would be reckless to gamble on the conclusions of the social scientists. We took the gamble with our eyes open, knowing our machinery for rent fixing would become completely clogged and unusable if we were wrong and any large proportion of the tenants tried to use it.

And one thing more. The Milner-Holland Committee throughout its report conscientiously attempted to destroy the over-simplified picture of innocent tenants trodden down by extortionate landlords. What they had discovered in London led them to the conclusion, not only that most tenants were living without a sense of grave injustice, but that good landlords who wanted to do repairs and improvements were paralysed by a tax system which denied them the concessions enjoyed by other forms of business. Any system of fair rents, the Committee concluded, would have to be fair to the landlord as well as to the tenant.

In addition to the reasons of common justice for this conclusion there was the glaring fact that vast twilight areas in our conurbations are rapidly and unnecessarily degenerating into slums because under present conditions the small landlord often cannot carry out the necessary maintenance and improvements. A good Rent Act must not provide a further obstacle in the way of overcoming this problem but help to solve it. In so far as the Act did this it is because it was based on the best available evidence.

central intelligence

I have one thing more to say about economic and social intelligence. If lack of it has for years been one of the major deficiencies of Whitehall, it is particularly damaging to a socialist government trying for the first time to introduce full-scale economic planning. Many of the mistakes we have made were due to our being compelled to plan without a sufficient basis of information, and if we are frank we must admit that however hard we work it will be some years before we get over this drawback.

We have, of course, begun to reorganise the work of the Central Statistical Department. When we came into power some eight years had elapsed since Mr. Macmillan's famous speech complaining about having to catch trains by last year's Bradshaw. It was in 1962 that the Tories repented about planning and NEDC was established. In these circumstances, one might have expected that the Government would find a duly strengthened Central Statistical Office tackling the basic problems, difficult as they are, of finding out something about current trends and changes and also about the structure of industry and social conditions. Both are needed to establish a sound tactical and strategical approach to our economic and social ills.

What we in fact found was profoundly disturbing. The most up to date information on inter-industry relationships (input-output tables) related to 1954. Little had been done by way of computerisation to speed up the processing of data collected more recently—for example the 1963 Census of Production. Even now we remain in the dark about even such elementary things as population movements, although the 1961 Census of Population is by now very out of date—even though it has not yet all been published. Balance of payments statistics, crucial for formulating economic policy, were subject to vast amendments years after the time to which they related. The figures of the 1951 crisis, for instance, were completely changed in character by amendments. The national income—a basic figure if ever there was one—is calculated in three different ways which yield three different results. Sometimes these differences are greater than the size of the change one is interested in. Another example is that we did not even have figures for the weekly movement of balances in and out of London, and thus could never catch up with one of the most important problems, that of the capital balance. Employment statistics were months behind and extremely unreliable. So were statistics on earnings.

We have begun to tackle all this. The number of high posts in our statistical services has been substantially increased. We have shifted the Social Survey into a central department so as to be able to make full use of it. A new head of the Central Statistical Office has been appointed. Though it takes years to improve census reports we are urgently strengthening the personnel and we are on the way to getting more speedy and accurate facts.

What about departmental as distinct from central research? In the Ministry of Housing I found a great deal of research going on, some of it by mixed teams of sociologists, architects, administrators and planners. The personnel was excellent but the more I saw of their work the more dubious I became about Ministries running anything but short term investigations. For one thing, when it comes to drafting a report the conclusions are nearly always emasculated by the time it gets anywhere near the Minister. But it was not only the conclusions that suffered under the process of editing and re-editing which took place as the document climbed up the hierarchy. The report itself was bound to lose the provocative cutting edge of the first draft. As it ascended the ranks of seniority, each Civil Servant decided that on balance it was safer to leave out this troublesome passage, that graphic phrase. I am inclined to believe that while Whitehall certainly needs greatly improved methods of collecting and ordering information, most medium term inquiries are best produced by Universities and outside research institutions working for Ministries under research contracts. In long term research I am sure this is the relationship we should normally encourage.

That is why, in the Ministry of Housing, we managed, with the help of the Ford Foundation, to get somewhere in the region of about £1 million for the establishment of a new Institute of Environmental Studies. This body, though it will have representatives of Whitehall on its board, will be completely independent. Its task will be to have an oversight of the research that is going on, particularly in British Universities; to be aware of the research requirements of the Ministries concerned with the built environment and so to feed out, particularly to our new social science departments in the new Universities, research contracts. These will relate not to the short term problems of the Government (these are best covered by Governmental institutions) but to medium and long term problems. The Institute, I am glad to say, is established and its trustees are on the point of appointing its first Director. It should form a model for a number of similar institutions providing the right nexus between Government intelligence requirements and the world of research.

Of course, it will take time before the changes I have described yield concrete results. What I can claim is that more has been done since 1964 to cope with the shortage of information of which Professor Townsend complains than was achieved in the whole period of Conservative rule.

civil servants and elections

I now turn to the second problem which a Labour Government faces. How to employ the Civil Service and the Government machine as instruments of social change. This, of course, is a hoary topic of debate in socialist circles. During the long years of opposition we saw it from outside government. Now we are looking at it from inside, and I think we can see rather more clearly the problems involved in using Whitehall as an instrument of social change.

Some of the difficulties we foresaw are very much smaller than I at least anticipated. Take for instance the fear that many socialists still feel that the Civil Service will resist socialist legislation. Broadly speaking I would say that it is quite untrue to believe that Whitehall, if you are firmly committed to anything, would try to stop you doing it. It is my experience that if they know you are determined to do any simple, easily understood, specific measure—they will do it for you with knobs on. Civil Servants are careful people. They have re-insurance policies, they study the Opposition as carefully as they study the Government and that is why they are always ready for you when you cease to be Opposition and become Government. My Ministry had been at work for months on a contingency plan for carrying out the section of our manifesto relating to housing.

So what most Socialists still imagine will be the main problem facing the Labour Government simply is not a problem. Of course your Civil Servants will argue about the exact way of putting your plans into practice. That is their job and any politician should be grateful. But as for the idea that Whitehall is afraid of the jolt caused by a change of Government and is against the prospect of new men with new ideas, I can only give my impression that Civil Servants not only acquiesce in the inevitable—some of them are glad at the prospect of a shakeup in the political stratosphere and quite often complain that the new man does not have enough new ideas.

So in the areas of what you might call legislative change the limiting factor is certainly not any resistance by the Civil Service. A far more important limiting factor is the chronic shortage of Parliamentary draftsmen. This is certainly the worst bottleneck we experienced in 1964 and it still remains far the most powerful brake on legislative reform. The Parliamentary draftsman is the rarest and most valuable species of human being in Whitehall. It takes many years to mature them and each is a unique virtuoso and a law unto himself. The men responsible for drafting the Bills can be counted on the fingers of both hands. And it is this chronic, desperate shortage of draftsmen which is the biggest obstacle delaying a Government intent on legislating social change. That so little attention is paid to this fact, in books written about the Constitution and the working of politics shows how remote the academic student of politics often is from the life of Whitehall.

administrative resistance to change

So far I have talked exclusively about legislation—the area where change is easiest for a reforming Government. If reform were merely a matter of passing laws and issuing Orders in Council then a socialist government would find most of the obstacles in its way not in Whitehall but across the road in the Palace of Westminster. But, of course, legislation is only a part, and in modern life the less important part, of Reform. Whether we look at the problems of change from the point of view of the Cabinet, as a corporate unity, or of the individual departmental minister, it is obvious that the extent of change and the rate of change depend far more on ad-

82

ministration than on legislation and it is in this field—the management of departments, the control of the nationalised industries, the supervision of local government—that the fate of any reforming government, and of each individual reforming minister, is decided.

When you have studied Whitehall and written and talked about it for years it is fascinating suddenly to be inside. I would like to mention four of the sharpest impressions made upon me in those first months.

circulation of the elites

Before the election I wondered whether Dr. Balogh in his contribution to *The Establishment* had not exaggerated the importance of the Lloyd George minute in 1918. Now I am quite sure he did not. That minute under which the head of the Treasury became the head of the Civil Service, and all appointments of Permanent Secretaries and Deputy Secretaries were transferred to him and the Prime Minister, really did begin the administrative revolution in Whitehall. Under the old rule Permanent Secretaries were normally bred in their own departments. Since they were specialists the difference at least at the top between the administrator and the professional was far less marked. The Lloyd George minute not only centralised power and patronage thus beginning the development towards Prime Ministerial Government; it also produced a new kind of Permanent Secretary—a professional administrator ready to cope with any department at a moment's notice and nearly always wearing that demeanour which connotes a period of service in the Treasury. The one expertise which these new Permanent Secretaries all share is skill in operating the Whitehall system and handling politicians. It is for the historian and the social scientist to study this change and to tell us whether the circulation of elites which produces this new breed of mandarins has improved the flexibility and efficiency of Whitehall. For the incoming politician there are advantages in having their peculiar expertise available. But this is offset by the difficulty he finds in avoiding being altogether cut off by the administrative embrace from contact with the specialists and professionals who know and care about the causes he has at heart.

stratification and hierarchy

I entered Whitehall with a strong prejudice against both these phenonema. That prejudice has not been eased. I never thought much of Plato's idea of a three class state divided into *Guardians* at the top, making all the wise decisions. *Auxiliaries* in the middle, administering the decisions, and Craftsmen at the bottom, doing all the donkey work. If I dislike that system even as an idea laid up in the heaven of Platonic dialogue, I like it no more when I find it enmeshed in the mundane realities of Whitehall. You do not get the best out of human beings by any kind of administrative apartheid. As for the hierarchy of responsibility within each department, I am only going to say that it puts severe limitations on an active minister wanting to move forward along the whole of the front that he controls.

The extreme centralisation of the hierarchy is, of course, a direct result of the theory (or is it a myth?) of ministerial responsibility. In order to keep the monarchy constitutionally responsible for everything, we arranged that it could do no wrong—and thereby made it impotent to do anything at all. Under our present system in Whitehall there is a danger of ministers going the way of monarchs. Indeed we already have a fantastic degree of bureaucratic centralisation without the compensating advantage of an effective ministerial responsibility to Parliament.

Certainly centralisation has its very considerable practicable disadvantages. As Minister of Housing for example I felt I had to answer the very large number of letters sent to me personally which enter the Ministry each day. I was told that this was not the normal practice and when I insisted I was warned that it would impose an unbearable burden on me since every letter I signed constituted a decision for which the Department as a whole was responsible. After many months a compromise was achieved which the Department found tolerable. It was only some time later that I discovered the reasons for its tenacious resistance to what seemed a commonsensical ministerial request. If most of the correspondence directed to the Minister is taken over by the Department the answers can be dealt with by an Executive Officer. But if the Minister insists on dealing with it himself then the draft, which starts at the bottom, must pass right up the hierarchy with officer after officer doing his best to improve it. And that means a lot more work not only for the Minister but for everyone else. I very soon discovered that if a minister tries to do more than a certain amount the whole hierarchical structure is in danger of breaking down. As at present constituted Departments can only tolerate a limited amount of simultaneous change. I very much hope that the Fulton Committee (which has undertaken the most important survey into the Civil Service since Stafford Northcote in 1866) will look into these twin issues of stratification and hierarchy very carefully and ask whether either of them is essential to the organisation of a modern Department of State.

the platonic idea in Whitehall

The third factor I want to mention derives from the previous two. Most of us, I suppose, know in private life the feeling that a letter which has been unanswered for two days may as well stay unanswered for two weeks, and once it has been unanswered that long it can surely stay there for ever. Because Whitehall is a closed system which combines the highest standard of integrity with a passion for procedures (as distinct from the results that derive from them) it is always bound to be in danger of succumbing to this kind of timelessness. I soon found it very difficult to eradicate from my mind the impression that everything in my red box would remain outside time until I had signed the document and my private secretary had then put the date on it and let it back into the world. In this closed society of dedicated administrators, problems very soon become detached from the real world where they originated. What was once a desperately urgent problem is snatched out of tempestuous reality into the calm of Whitehall and stays floating there until, in due course, it is picked up, dealt with and re-enters time again. This kind of timelessness makes it difficult sometimes to get the pace of action in government departments required in an age of rapid social change.

new ministries for old

During our years of opposition we spent a great deal of time and trouble discussing Government structure and deciding how the departments could best be re-organised in order to serve the interests of *The National Plan*. Our main decision was to create a brand new Ministry of Planning and so the Prime Minister announced the formation of the DEA. When you introduce major changes of this kind into a Civil Service as hierarchical as ours they cause a gigantic disturbance. Indeed one of the lessons of our first Parliament was that in view of the short-term damage you do by any change of Government structure you must be very sure of the long-term returns before you start it. I am one of those who is completely convinced that we had to set the DEA alongside the Treasury. How else could we hope to achieve either a National Prices and Incomes Policy or a National Plan. Of course the creation of the DEA caused acute tensions because it shattered old prejudices and upset the old balance of prestige. But if you are going to introduce effective overall planning you are going to cause problems anyway; and the Department you specially create for this purpose will be detested and distrusted if officials feel that it deprives them of power. In Britain two years is a very short time in which to get a brand new central Ministry working well.

Another example of these difficulties is the Ministry of Technology. I was sitting beside Harold Wilson when he made his announcement about the future of the Ministry of Aviation. Suddenly I remembered my first speech as shadow Minister of Science. We had all got together in the Bloomsbury Hotel and after lengthy arguments with our scientific and technological advisers we had agreed that under the next Labour Government the Ministry of Aviation must be split up; the defence aspects should go to the Ministry of Defence and the production side to the new Ministry of Technology we were determined to create. Well it has taken two years hard fighting in Whitehall to achieve the formal announcement of the change we had so gaily decided on. Even now the main job is still to be done.

Professor Abel-Smith is sure we ought to have done all this much faster. All I can say is that if it has taken time at least we haven't been deflected by all the obstacles from the vision we had in those far-away days of opposition. If we had more difficulties with the Ministry of Land and Natural Resources, at least it launched the two important pieces of legislation consigned to it—and that would have been impossible without a special ministry. Reforming Government structure is a tough assignment. If you do it directly you arrive in Whitehall, fresh from opposition, you may well find efficiency has been decreased by some of your efforts to improve it. But if you wait and test your ideas in Whitehall the prevailing inertia will soon dampen your initial impetus into a spent force. That is why it was right to make these changes early.

reform of parliament and local government

I have spoken so far as if, in shaping the instruments of social change, our only difficulties were in Whitehall. But we had difficulties elsewhere. In the House of Commons for example. Since Parliament is hardly an ideal instrument of social change we had to work at a strategy of parliamentary reform. In the first Parliament we didn't get very far. Even now, with a splendid new intake of young Members (they started at least, enthusiastic for reform) we are not getting very far very fast. However we have now opened a first modest package of parliamentary reform, including the first two Specialist Committees one on agriculture and the other on science and technology and a trial run of morning sittings.

Some socialists are still deeply convinced that the kind of Parliamentary reform we require consists of strengthening the executive and weakening the legislature still further. I believe they are wrong and that it will stimulate the executive and improve its quality if we remove some of the myths which at present conceal the weakness of Parliament and the power of Whitehall in order to equip the former with strengthened powers of investigation. But I also feel that if the Parliament's authority should be revived, the executive's ability to obtain essential legislation speedily also needs strengthening. I am frankly sceptical whether the present method of examining Bills in Standing Committees achieves results justified by the days and sometimes nights of word-spinning often involved. I wonder whether the Finance Bill, which stifles each summer session into protracted boredom, should not be dealt with in Committee and not on the floor of the House. But I am also profoundly aware that a really comprehensive reform of Parliament (including the House of Lords as well as the House of Commons, and knitting the two together) will take time. We shall be lucky if by the end of this Parliament the job is three-quarters done.

And then there is local government where the need for a complete overhaul, a re-constitution in fact, in newer and bigger units, is now virtually uncontested. Three years ago it was commonly said that one thing no Cabinet could dare to commit itself to was local government reform. Today those who care most about local government, officials and elected representatives, are keenest in recommending drastic policies to the Royal Commission. I think we can claim some credit for the creation of this atmosphere. But again the reform will take time. Even if things go well we can hardly expect the Bill to be presented before the first year of the next Parliament; and after it is on the Statute Book there will probably be at least two years before the appointed day. So the modern dynamic local government we all desire is maybe five years off and meanwhile in carrying through our social reforms we must make do with the jostling chaos of county and county boroughs, the medley of efficiency and inefficiency which was accepted as inevitable and unalterable until this Labour Government was elected.

So my first reply to the central criticism contained in the first three lectures is to say that two years is too short a period in which to judge a Socialist Government's record of social reform. After thirteen years of opposition we were bound to find our programme held up by quite a number of formidable obstacles. These obstacles do not include resistance by the Civil Service to legislative change. Quite the contrary! What they do include is:

1. the need to make good deficiencies in the collection, assessment and dissemination of intelligence throughout Whitehall.

2. the need to reform the structure of Whitehall even at the cost of short term delay.

3. the need to adapt anachronistic Parliamentary procedures to the pace of modern social change.

4. unavoidable reliance in all the main services on a structure of local government almost unchanged since the horse and buggy age.

5. the necessity, while reshaping all these basic institutions of democratic life, to deal with immediate economic and social problems even though this means using the old blunt instruments we inherited from our predecessors.

the central issue : which socialist priorities ?

In the first part of this essay I described some of the problems which faced us when we took over in October 1964 after nearly 13 years of opposition. Committed to an ambitious programme we were bound to spend much of our energies on legislation and administrative reorganisation of which the benefits could not be felt for some years. But while we were fashioning the new instruments of social change we also had to grapple with the emergency we inherited as well as introducing a whole series of short term rescue operations which were bound to embarrass or retard our long term reforms.

These short term measures have received some rough handling in the previous lectures. In dealing with these criticisms I must start by making explicit a basic disagreement about socialist strategy. "The Government . . . has allowed itself to be diverted from giving priority to poverty into giving priority to redeployment." (p61) Peter Townsend remarks and Brian Abel-Smith elaborates the same theme, "While it is undoubtedly true that correcting the balance of payments is an essential aim and failure to do so could lead to mass unemployment, it is by no means certain that social justice welfare and better social capital depend upon rapid growth of the economy. The ugly gap between private affluence and public squalor could be corrected without economic growth." (pp15-16)

Let it be quite clear what our critics are saying. They censure the Labour Government for giving first priority to industrial growth and relating its plans for expanding the social services to the planned expansion of the national wealth. If I understand it aright, their contention is that though it is obviously convenient to have a growth rate sufficient to ensure that social services can be improved without increased taxation it is not essential, since a Socialist must regard social security mainly as a means of economic re-distribution. Not only must we strive to alter the balance between the public and the private sector to the advantage of the public but we must also use pension schemes and family allowances, for example, in order to redistribute income between the social classes. If this is not given a high priority in socialist planning, they argue, the gap between private affluence and public squalor may actually widen during a period of successful expansion.

Of course the danger they point to is a real one especially in prosperous democratic societies where poverty is frequently concentrated in the poorly organised and electorally less significant sectors of the population. Of course, it is also true that a socialist government must constantly strive to achieve a fairer distribution of the national wealth. Nevertheless it seems to me that the strategy recommended in the earlier lectures is both unrealistic and completely inconsistent with the Labour Government's Election Manifesto. If there was one theme central to that Manifesto it was the contention that higher living standards and improved social services could only be achieved by obtaining a steady and continuous expansion of the national income. So, well before we took office, the Labour Party was committed to giving planned expansion top priority, and relating the speed with which we introduced our social reforms to the rate of growth we achieved.

It seems to me rather absurd to attack the Government because it has not abandoned the central theme of its election programme. Indeed it would be more reasonable to attack us for departing from our strategy and accepting the critics' view that poverty must be dealt with whether the economy is expanding or not. One of the first acts of the Government in November 1964 was to finance a large increase in old age pensions and abolition of the prescription charges out of increased taxation. In terms of the defence of the pound and economic expansion these concessions to the old and the sick were dangerously large. We made them because we agreed with Abel-Smith and Townsend that our first big attack on poverty could not be postponed however strong the economic reasons for doing so might be.

Nor was this a single isolated action. First in July 1965 and then again in 1966 the Cabinet decided that the restrictions and cuts required to overcome our economic difficulties should not be permitted to affect our priority social programmes. It is interesting to see how this decision was treated by our critics. Brian Abel-Smith says that he appreciates that " social expenditure has on the whole been kept as planned, with the result that the cut is falling on private investment and private consumption. But it is hardly satisfactory to define as a socialist someone who preserves the social services when times are hard " (p16). Well, well! I should have thought it was the mark of a socialist to make sure that the sacrifices required in an economic crisis do not fall on the weakest sections of the community and do not affect the Government's social priorities. In fact what distinguishes our discriminating socialist deflation from Tory stop-go is firstly that the squeeze was accompanied by an overall freeze affecting prices as well as incomes, and secondly that our squeeze was selective sparing all our priority social programmes whereas theirs was across the board. Fair shares in adversity is as relevant a definition of socialism as fair shares in affluence.

overcoming the crisis

In the last paragraph of his essay Brian Abel-Smith remarks quietly " It is true that the present economic crisis has been ignored in this discussion. But with luck the crisis should be over in a few months." (p24) That he can write in this way illustrates clearly enough that gap I mentioned between the socialist academic and the practical politician. Throughout our first two years the balance of payments crisis—sometimes in the background, sometimes in the foreground—was with the Government day in, day out and its solution accepted as priority number one. I am not going to waste time arguing who was to blame for this crisis; but since Professor Abel-Smith has compared the proposed rate of spending under the National Plan with the actual rate of spending in the last period of Tory rule I must call attention to one relevant aspect of the crisis. We not only inherited the external consequences of an election spending spree of quite inordinate proportions. Even more serious we took over Departments geared to a Conservative four years spending programme to which the country had been committed without any proper consideration of the relation between public sector growth and private sector growth. Local authorities were encouraged to work out ambitious expansion plans—more roads, more houses, more hospitals, more schools—combined with fantastic projects of central redevelopment. The Army, the Navy and the Air Force, not to mention the aircraft industry, were equally firmly committed to fantastic plans of expansion, worked out apparently without any consideration of the amount of the national income that would be absorbed year by year. One of the first and most painful tasks of the Government was to bring these gigantic plans of public expenditure under control, to assess their relative priorities and to relate them rationally to the national income. It was not an easy task—especially for a Labour Government. In order to give a fair judgement one must surely measure our economy measures against the background of the chronic balance of payments crisis we have had to overcome and the Tory electoral spending jamboree which was its cause.

the role of the prices and incomes policy

In overcoming it we have been forced to experiment in quite novel socialist measures —in particular the prices and incomes policy. I needn't dilate at length on what happened. The attempt to work a voluntary policy on which we embarked was obviously not succeeding last summer and we were forced into the temporary expedient of an absolute standstill. Without doubt the most important task we face in the coming year is to do our utmost to work out a method which will, if possible, be acceptable to both sides of industry for keeping increases in income in line with the increase in real national output.

But what, you may ask, has the prices and incomes policy got to do with the war against poverty with which our three critics are almost exclusively concerned? My answer to this question is that Prices and Incomes Policy is not merely an essential tool of socialist economic planning; it also has a vital role to play in the battle against poverty. Though the Tories announced their belief in a policy of this kind and, indeed, made some efforts to introduce one, they were completely unsuccessful because they failed to realise that it cannot be considerd solely in terms of economic criteria. The social programme of the Government, as expressed particularly in its budgets, forms an essential background to any prices and incomes policy. If it disregards social justice and redistributive justice it will not carry the trade union movement. And the converse of this is true. Our war against poverty cannot be waged in isolation from the rest of our economic policy. Indeed it must be regarded as a carefully balanced part of the total overall plan (including the prices and incomes element) which we present to the nation. It is because the three preceding essays completely overlook this connection that they seem so curiously remote from everyday reality.

waging the war against poverty

Let me now turn to what is really the hub of the critics' argument. Have we done enough since we took over to improve the living standards of the poorest section of the community? As socialists, of course, we realised that the inequalities in income and wealth which we found when we took over two years ago, are far too wide. True, the overall extent of poverty has been enormously reduced by economic expansion since the war, but the intensity of poverty in the midst of affluence has probably actually increased. We cannot rely on economic forces to reduce the gap. We have to take deliberate action. It won't happen by itself. Indeed the present degree of inequality is the direct result of market forces being left to determine wages, salaries and profits throughout the whole period since the Tories took over in 1951 and "set the country free from socialist controls."

What kind of decisions are these which have to be taken? Partly they are governmental decisions about the distribution of the tax burden. But there are limits to the amount of redistribution which can be achieved over the short-term by taxation.

It is right, therefore, that the prices and incomes policy should be developed so that it plays a part in achieving our goal. This involves working for the reduction of prices which yield excessive profits. It also requires that better paid workers should be willing to let the lowest paid workers get a better share in rising productivity, even if this narrows the differential. As we have seen, an effective prices and incomes policy ultimately depends on the self-discipline of both sides of industry. In fact we can neither contain inflation without stop-go nor yet wage the war against poverty in affluence, without a social and moral revolution in our attitudes to collective bargaining and a free market.

That is yet another reason for dismissing as unrealistic the Townsend, Abel-Smith assertion that "the gap between private affluence and public squalor could be corrected without economic growth." In war time it is just possible to persuade democratic communities to accept the fair shares of a rationed siege economy and even to welcome the drastic restrictions and heavy sacrifices involved. But this readiness to share is only "for the duration." As the Attlee Cabinet discovered, a Government suspected of prolonging rationing and restrictions further than necessary courts electoral defeat. Indeed I am prepared to assert against our critics that in peacetime the gap between private affluence and public squalor *cannot* be corrected without a fairly rapid rate of economic growth. In an economic crisis people will be prepared to accept restrictions, self-sacrifice and even a degree of redundancy. But there is a severe limit both in time and in extent to the restrictions which are acceptable.

haphazard skirmishes—or reform by stages

I now turn to the detailed criticisms of our social programme. Peter Townsend writes "What was planned to be a consistent and concerted attack on poverty has turned into haphazard skirmishes on a wide front" and he goes on to complain, "The Government has given little impression from its actions that it has adopted an overall strategy. By increasing benefits along conventional lines early in 1965 it took the edge off demands for reform. By then introducing a redundancy payments Act and later earnings related benefit in unemployment and sickness for the first six months, it allowed itself to be diverted from giving priority to poverty to giving priority to redeployment." (p61). Professor Townsend then asks "What has happened to . . . the wage related scheme of social security incorporating national superannuation? I believe it can be argued that with a little more determination on the part of the Government we might have had this on the Statute Book by the end of 1965." (p60).

Let me deal with this point by point. Were we wrong to give the flat rate increase in November 1964? Of course we realised that this would "take the edge off demands for reform" that is it would reduce the amount of misery which we inherited. Surely it is a little cold-blooded to suggest that we should have deliberately preserved this misery in order to keep an effective demand for radical reform. It may be true that the flat-rate increase "took the edge off the demand for reform" by making the introduction of national superannuation appear less immediately urgent. But in any event a scheme of the size and nature which we contemplate could not by any stretch of imagination have been on the Statute Book by the end of 1965. I still think we were right to give the immediate relief we had promised priority over our long-term reforms.

Professor Townsend also rebukes us for our decision to move from a flat-rate system to a graded system by stages—for introducing redundancy payments and unemployment and sickness benefits first and leaving earnings related pensions for a second stage. I disagree with him profoundly. If we had failed to provide the redundancy payments and the earnings related benefits before this winter began, we should have been guilty of making no provision for those who have suffered redundancy as a result of the July measures. Even though the unemployment figures have not soared to the heights predicted so confidently by our critics, we all of us detest the level they have reached. Personally I am thankful that instead of trying to reform Beveridge in one single huge leap forward we decided to do it in stages. By so doing we have made life a good deal less intolerable for those who have taken the knock. We have also, by another of our measures, namely the introduction of the supplementary benefits scheme, set non-contributory benefits on a new course and provided additional help, particularly for old people. Finally on this I would like to remove any suspicions our critics may have that national superannuation has not only been postponed but abandoned. This Labour Government keeps its pledges as the last one did. We promised to reform the Beveridge system by introducing earnings related social security including old age pensions. We shall keep that promise and have the reform on the Statute Book in the lifetime of this Parliament.

family endowment—the gaping hole

I now turn to the second main social problem they discuss—the disturbing concentration of poverty today among large families. And here I must make a confession. In our long period of opposition we failed as a party to grapple with this problem nearly as thoroughly as we grappled with the rest of social security. The working party of which our three critics were members, did start on the discussion of how to reform the family allowances. But we never got our ideas into a form workable enough for presentation to annual conference. That, of course, is why the subject was scarcely mentioned in the 1964 election programme. Our experience in Government brought home the seriousness of the situation so that in the 1966 Manifesto we got a bit further, "We shall establish a Ministry of Social Security . . . It will deal with the whole range of social security questions and ensure a rational single system of paying benefits. The Ministry will also head a drive to seek out and alleviate poverty, whether among children or old people. Finally in the interests of greater equity we shall seek ways of integrating more fully the two quite different systems of social payments—tax allowances and cash benefits paid under National Insurance." (Time for decision p15)

Vague as it was this was the first commitment the Labour Party made to a revision of children's allowances and the first recognition of the thesis Professor Titmuss has so brilliantly argued that tax allowances are middle class social security. The commitment to deal with the family problem was made considerably more specific in the recent White Paper, *Prices and Incomes*—The period of severe restraint (HMSO, 1966) Paragraph 28 runs, "Lowest Paid Workers. Improvement of the standard of living of the worst-off members of the community is a primary social objective. As in practice the needs of individual workers are largely determined by the extent of their family commitments, the Government will continue to give a high priority to measures specifically designed to meet family needs." I needn't tell our three friends that these words were put into the White Paper very carefully. The significance of the paragraph is that the problem about which they feel so passionately is fully recognised by the Government. I only wish that in those long years of opposition we had got round to working out a blue-print for family endowments because now it is obvious that this is the yawning gap in our social security system: the area of greatest poverty is covered with the least adequate social provision. They are right to launch a crusade with the object of rousing the public conscience in the face of the poverty so widespread among large families. They are right to urge on the Government the need for imaginative new policies which grapple with this complex issue. Where they are wrong, I am pretty sure, is in the oversimplified device which they provide as an answer.

Well that is the end of my reply to the specific complaints of our three critics. So let me return in conclusion to their main contention that we have lost our way, our strategy has collapsed and our short-term rescue measures are largely ineffective. My first reply is that it is just too early to judge. We have been two and a half years in office and we have four more years to run. I hope they won't think me complacent, but when I look back at the 1964 Parliament I am still genuinely surprised that with a majority of three in Parliament and a major economic crisis to cope with, we achieved as much progress as we did in carrying out the programme of our election Manifesto. In order to demonstrate this I have selected in this lecture two sections of the Manifesto—one, in which I have been particularly concerned, housing, and the other, in which the critics were particularly concerned, social security. On both these sectors of the front I have shown that in fact we have made far more progress than the tone of their criticism suggests.

On other sectors, the Health Service and education, for example, I could have told a similar story. The main area of disappointment was one they hardly mentioned, the voluntary Prices and Incomes Policy to which we were pledged and which we were compelled last July to supercede temporarily with a total standstill. This is the one sector where we have been compelled to depart from our plans and resort to methods not included in our electoral Mandate. But on the sector which they care about most, social security and the war against poverty, there has been, not a failure of a policy to which we were committed, but the postponed implementation of a long-term plan in order to carry out a short-term relief operation. Stage by stage we are carrying out the policy we worked out in Opposition as well as filling in the gaping hole left by our failure to work out a blue-print for family endowment. I would not have thought that, with this new Parliament only one year old, this is the situation where old friends outside in the Universities should start wringing their hands and jumping to defeatist conclusions. I myself feel no doubt that we shall, in the lifetime of this Parliament, complete the task we set ourselves in Opposition of breaking away from Beveridge and creating a system of social security which abolishes poverty in affluence.